The Harmony of Bill Evans

by Jack Reilly

Originally published by Unichrom Ltd. and distributed by Hal Leonard Corporation

ISBN 978-0-7935-3152-3

7777 W. Bluemound Rd. P.O. Box 13819 Milwaukee, WI 53213

Visit Hal Leonard Online at
www.halleonard.com

AUTHOR'S NOTES

Except for "Time Remembered," Modal and Intervallic Analyses, all of these articles originally appeared in LETTER FROM EVANS, a quarterly newsletter dedicated to the memory of Bill Evans. I served on the Board of Advisors for three years. Subsequent to my resignation, I decided to revise and enlarge the originals and to publish them in book form, hoping to reach a larger audience.

Nenette Evans, Bill Evans' widow, was a great encouragement in the early stages of this project, and I wish to thank her for that. Through her kindness, I came in contact with many people who are dedicated and committed to the legacy of her late husband.

Several colleagues made material available, both music and articles, and I should like to acknowledge Krey L. Jilca, author and president of Unichrom; Sean Petrahn, author and critic at large, for contributing his penetrating essay on "The Education of the Jazz Musician"; and Jean M. Browne, president of Apple Music Copy Services, for her intelligence, kindness and tireless effort in the preparation of the music examples and presentation of this book.

For their reading of the manuscript and expert proof reading, I am indebted to Mrs. Anne Toolajian, Ms. Arca Nilol, Clara Hamra, Camille Fredrickson, Marty Murphy, Al Schoonmaker, and Henry Okstel.

I owe thanks above all to my student and dear friend of long standing, Loren Toolajian. Without his persistence, leadership, and ideas, this book would not have come to fruition. Lastly, to Tom Mykityshyn for his generosity, and to my wife Carol for her abundant love, comfort and trust.

Sean Petrahn's article is courtesy of THE MUSIC BOX.

"Art is the creative custodianship of the truth."

Martin Heidegger

CONTENTS

PREFACE

Composing is the highest calling for a musician. Performing, whether it be interpreting or improvising, always takes second place. The musician in the 20th century, compared to one in the 16th century, is in a unique position; at his disposal are the great compositions of the past 400 years. The inheritance is prodigious. Bach didn't have Mozart or Beethoven; Mozart and Beethoven didn't have Brahms or Schumann; Schumann and Brahms didn't have Schoenberg, Berg, Webern, Boulez, Stockhausen, Carter, Bernstein, Gershwin, Copland, Barber, Ellington, or Bill Evans.

Jazz music is a players' (improvisers') art. The written or composed parts used in jazz performances are always subservient to the solo (improvised) sections. The Herman Herds are memorable because of the soloists (improvisers). Stan Getz's solo on "Early Autumn" will far outlast the song itself, as will Lester Young's solos with the Basie band, Ben Webster with Duke, Earl Hines, and Charlie Parker. Jazz is most exciting and exhilarating when played by a soloist, or in a duo, trio, quartet, or quintet setting. In order to fully develop as an improviser, the jazz musician, like the classical musician, must also play in large ensembles. But the real commitment and challenge that faces the jazz player comes when he is alone with his instrument. He must sit (or stand) with that instrument and improvise hour after hour, day after day, year after year, with NO LET UP! He or she must be convinced that there will always be a deeper level of creativity that has not yet been tapped. He or she must have the faith of Saints that these deeper levels will be reached, sometimes by leaps but mostly in upward spirals. He or she must sense, feel, and visualize a light shining inside the body and mind that grows ever brighter as each new level is mastered; and only when that light completely engulfs one during a performance will he or she know the meaning of Joy: a joy beyond description, one that will be felt by all, and that Joy shall be called MAGIC.

Bill Evans had Magic. He was a Magician on the highest plane of consciousness. He knew all music; all 400 years. He chose to develop and express his Magic through the art of jazz improvisation. He made a name for himself both as a soloist and with his trio. He was an interpreter of the American popular song. His improvisations were based on the Blues, Song Form, and Free Form structures. Historians and musicians have already acknowledged him as one of jazz's great innovators, but it may be a while before they rank him as one of America's great jazz composers.

The purpose of these analytical essays on Evans' compositions, including his standard repertoire, is threefold:

1. to give the jazz musician and the enlightened public insight into the compositional process;
2. to inspire jazz musicians and the enlightened public to play and learn his music; and
3. to reveal the depth and richness of his compositions, for they are <u>organic</u>, and therefore <u>complete</u>. There is absolutely no need to change a note, chord, or rhythm in any of his

works. Evans never wrote a tune, a melody, or a riff over someone else's chord progression. He did not consider that the art of composing. Nor do I.

A composer worthy of the name conceives and hears ideas in his mind's ear. These ideas will eventually be worked out on manuscript paper. A composer worthy of the name knows how to work these ideas on paper through a complete study of harmony, counterpoint, analysis, compositional forms, arranging, and orchestration. A composer worthy of the name is constantly developing and cultivating his sensitivity to the inner creative impulses so as to recognize them when they arrive. Then he/she takes—makes!—the time to think, sketch, write, and experiment on manuscript paper so the ideas will find outer form. The composer worthy of the name then completes these sketches and experiments into full-blown compositions. A man I nominate worthy of the name COMPOSER, is Bill Evans.

Jack Reilly
November 21, 1992
Park Slope, Brooklyn
New York, U.S.A.

THE EDUCATION OF THE JAZZ MUSICIAN

by Sean Petrahn

The shelves of all the major book stores house at least one volume devoted to the evolution of jazz, this uniquely American folk phenomenon. I will not attempt, therefore, to create a curriculum that necessarily complements or parallels the importance and influence of the leading figures of each era in jazz found in the history books. Rather, I shall boil it down to two major talents.

The evolution of jazz from 1890 to 1980 can be summed up in the music of two pianists: Art Tatum and Bill Evans. They are the towering figures who will outlast, historically, the Jelly Roll Mortons, the Duke Ellingtons, the Bud Powells, and even the Lennie Tristanos. That is to say, in the year 2080, only these two names need be mentioned in a jazz history course, because they were the synthesis of all that came before and all that will ever come after. Both men absorbed the innovations of not only the lesser piano talents (mentioned above), but also of the horn players: the Armstrongs, the Beiderbeckes, the Prezes, the Birds, the Zoots, the Getzs, and the Coltranes, those other interesting yet inevitably lower talents who forged the melodic paths of the jazz improvised line. Art Tatum and, more so, Bill Evans, also absorbed the music of the Western classical world, from Bach to Schoenberg, and any analysis of their styles must bring this to the fore.

What is it that makes jazz different from Western classical music? The answer is deceptively plain and simple. Jazz is almost totally improvised, while classical music is almost totally written down. Classical music is a *composer's* art: even the greatest geniuses and fastest-working composers in history—Johann Sebastian Bach, Wolfgang Amadeus Mozart, Gioacchino Rossini, Franz Schubert, Frederic Chopin, Hector Berlioz, Richard Strauss—took hours, days, or weeks to compose even so much as one minute's worth of music. And this is even true of those composers (Bach, Mozart, Chopin) who were known as great improvisers. Very little of their improvisations actually made it into their finished, published works; there was always some finishing or refining process that took place before their work went to the publisher.

Jazz, conversely, developed as an *improviser's* art. Despite the fact that there have been some very clever jazz composers and arrangers who formulated, in advance, introductions, main themes, bridges, and codas—Morton, Ellington, Eddie Sauter, George Handy, Thelonious Monk, and Charles Mingus spring immediately to mind—the principal interest in a jazz performance is *not* the pre-arranged formalities, any more than it is in a classical performance. The central crux of the listening experience is the manner in which themes are interwoven or developed. In classical music, this development is written down, while in jazz, it is improvised. There is no editing when you improvise; there is constant editing when you compose. In jazz, then, it takes exactly one minute to create one minute's worth of music...and therein lies the excitement, the danger, of playing jazz as opposed to playing classical music.

Despite this difference, there is (aside from the fact that both utilize Western musical forms and tonalities) one great similarity between the two musics. One learns to compose by imitating the best composers; one learns to improvise by imitating the best jazz improvisers. In other words, the quality of the present in music is always dependent, to some degree, on the quality of the past. It is implicit in this dictum that one learns how to play one's instrument in a virtuoso manner, before one can imitate Art Tatum or Bill Evans. One must be able to read (play) the masterworks before one can learn composition. In this light what, then, is the proper curriculum for the jazz student? Should there be a curriculum at all? Well, yes and no. Let's take a brief comparative historical look at Western music.

Jazz began when classical music had exhausted itself, circa 1910 - 1913; and if we isolate the elements of music (melody, harmony, and rhythm), we can—by comparison, analogy, and metaphor—gain a clearer picture of what I'm saying.

The modal (1100 - 1600 A.D.), tonal (1600 -1900 A.D.), and atonal (1900 - present) periods in Western music are arbitrary divisions that define and classify the way composers think, and organize their music. Each period created a synthesis of the previous one, and therefore generated more complex structures and vocabularies. This does not mean that I adhere totally to the Kantian principle of evolution, *i.e.*, that for each new stage or period there is a logical progression into the next, therefore, making it more complex. The motets of Gesualdo (modal period) were more complex than, say, Stravinsky's *Symphony of Psalms* (end of the tonal era). I like to think of each stage in musical evolution not as "progress" but as an unfolding gradually, layer by layer, of the total musical universe. A synthesis does create new problems in form, but also new possibilities. A composer living today has, indeed, much more to absorb and learn than one who lived in the 16th century, and therefore has greater demands placed on his artistic integrity in order to avoid rewriting the past. At the same time, however, he also has an enormous repertory from which to draw his inspiration. Each composer taps into a layer of the musical universe. The greater the genius, the clearer he translates his vision, and the greater demands he makes on the interpreter and listener.

The jazz improviser is limited by his technique. There is not one fraction of a second hesitation while improvising, otherwise he loses the "flow." It is a myth to think that an improviser hears internally more than he can play. It's always the other way around: you only create ideas that can be executed with precision; otherwise, you would stutter and stammer, hopelessly. NO mistakes are made when one improvises this way: mistakes mean that you are not hearing an idea internally. The hand is the medium of the message. The secret is that you only play what you can conceive in your mind's ear on the spur of the moment. Then improvising is easy, and technical development becomes the means to a greater end . . . and that greater end is ease, subtlety and eloquence in your playing.

The jazz curriculum is divided into three stages:

1. THE BLUES FORM
2. THE SONG FORM
3. THE FREE FORM

Each stage parallels the classifications mentioned above—modal, tonal, and atonal—with regard to the evolution of classical music. The Blues Form is *modal*, the Song Form is *tonal*, and the Free Form is *atonal*. This may appear an oversimplification, but categories and labels are necessary when one decides to teach such a vast area of musical thought. I like to think of each stage as paralleling the history of the human race, from *instinctive* to *intellectual* to the stage yet to come, *intuitive*. The student of jazz becomes reacquainted with this long process through the Blues Form (Instinctive), i.e. playing from the "gut" or solar plexus center. The Song Form engages the Intellect. This stage is more concerned with structure, key relationships, and harmony. The study of the Free Form (Intuitive) stage always comes last. The student, at this stage, should be a master improviser, his or her knowledge of the past now sunken into the unconscious mind, its function slightly analogous to a main-frame computer that stores billions of bits of information about a subject and its related topics (and subtopics, and subdivisions of subtopics). The student must then go through this experience, or rather process, from instinct to intellect to intuition, of improvising *at each stage in the curriculum*. For example, 1) he must try to improvise on the very basic blues structure—twelve bars, three scales, three chords—and in 4/4 meter, totally by *instinct, i.e.*, "feeling his way through," playing and making up melodies that sound good to him; 2) he must consciously learn and memorize the modes that can be applied to this basic twelve-bar structure, and on which he can experiment. This stage (and every stage) must be accompanied by listening to, and singing along with, the recordings of the improvisers playing the blues. This is *eartraining* and must also include the singing of the modes. 3) He must then "feel" and "know" that what was learned and memorized in Step 2 is second nature and fully absorbed by the unconscious. (I agree with Carl Jung that the unconscious mind is just as active, and probably more so than the conscious mind, and therefore continually digesting the information and readying it for use by the intuitive mind.) It is, in fact, in the *unconscious* mind that we develop understanding and wisdom. The sense or feeling of "second nature" cannot be defined, yet one knows it when it "arrives." And you know it through your playing. At the intuitive level of improvising, one has the feeling that one is NOT doing the playing; that someone else has taken over your mind, and is using YOUR hands to make music.

PERI'S SCOPE

HARMONIC ANALYSIS

"Peri's Scope" is a perfect model to initiate a discussion of two-handed piano voicing principles that are root oriented. There are three rules or directions to follow:

1. Use the root, third and seventh under the melody;
2. Omit the fifth of the chord;
3. For added, optional color, add a ninth, eleventh, or thirteenth

Observe in all of the examples that the root is always the bass note and above the root you place the third, seventh, and melody. The voice leading alternates—EX. 1: R (root), 3rd, 7th leading to R, 7th, 10th in measures 1 and 2; or R, 10th, 7th leading to R, 7th, 10th in measure 3—depending upon the root movement. In this tune the root movement is mostly down a fifth (or up a fourth, i.e. II–V, III–VI of measures 1 & 2). I call this the diatonic cycle of fifths, and since "Peri's Scope" does not modulate to another key, I rate it as a very imaginative diatonic composition for that reason. Bill had a composer's ear for variety and learned how to effectively use secondary dominants (see measures 7, 8, 14, 15, 16 & 20). This makes Peri's Scope a challenge to the improviser. The challenge is unique because you meet the secondary dominants in different ways and in different parts of the phrase.

For example, in EX. 2 below, the IIIx (E secondary dominant seventh) lasts for two bars (7 & 8) and it's the climax of the first phrase of the tune. It's very sudden. It jumps out at us.

From Bar 1 to 6 all we heard were diatonic chords in C Major, then "boom!", we're hit with an E7^{13} for two bars. A real surprise. Look at EX. 2 and see and hear the colors: E7^{13}, then E7^{b13}, then E7 and finally E7^{+11}!!

At the end of the second phrase (also eight measures), EX. 3 measures 14, 15 & 16, we meet three secondary dominants in a row, B7^{13} to E9^{+11} to A7^{13}!!! The alterations on the IIIx at measure 15 begin to look and sound like its tritone substitute, a B flat dominant seventh +5. It is at this point the improviser has a choice to use one or the other: an E9^{13} or Bb9^{+5}. Here the progression becomes chromatic if you use the Bb9 and remains diatonic if you use the E9^{11}.

In this second phrase, measures 14–16, the improviser has a choice to think diatonically by using B7 to E7 to A7, or chromatically B7 to Bb7 to A7. A chromatic progression is one in which the root of the chord lies outside the key signature of the tune. All others are diatonic progressions.

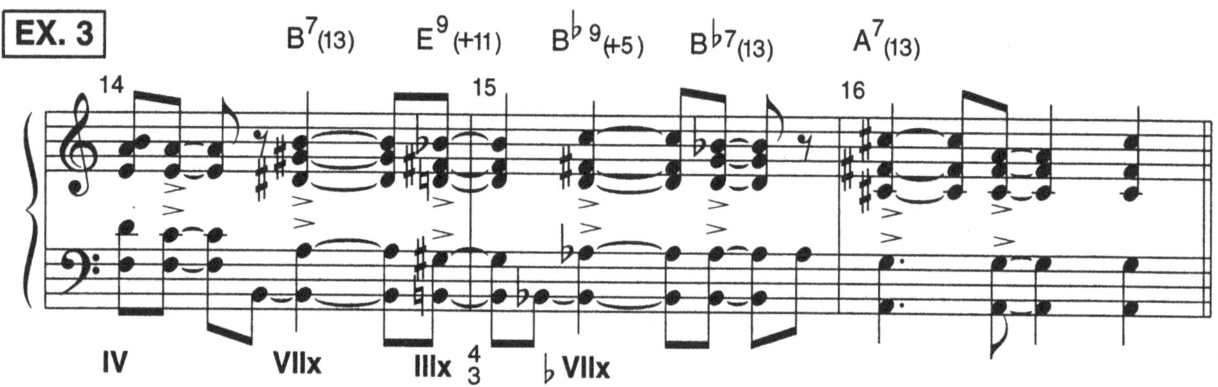

In phrase three, at bar 20 of the final eight measures (EX. 4), we meet a secondary dominant for one-half of the measure only. It is the VIx (A7^{b13}) again on the 3rd and 4th beats. In Bill's improvisation in this measure he plays B-flats, revealing to us that the chord on the downbeat of measure 20 is an E minor 7^{b5}, a III half-diminished. It is only implied in this arrangement. The symbol for half-diminished is ø. The symbol x stands for secondary dominant.

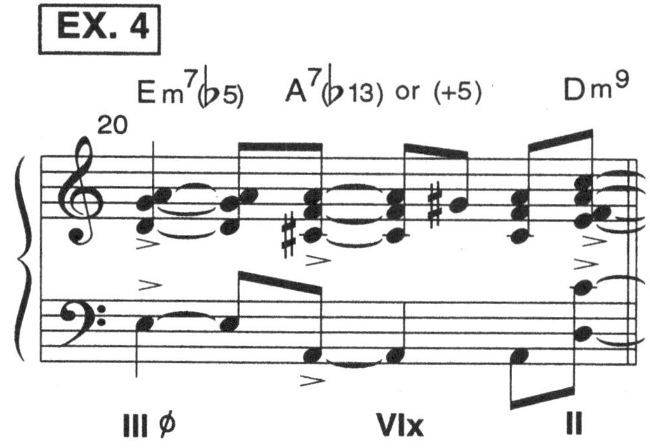

In EX. 5, we can see at a glance how imaginatively Bill used the secondary dominants in different parts of each phrase. Here's a look at the phrases by measure number. It will give you a quick overview of where the secondary dominants occur.

EX. 5

Peri's Scope

(Roman Numeral Analysis)

Phrase One (measures 1–8)

Dm7	G7	Em7	Am7	Dm7	G7	CMa7	Am7
II	V	III	VI	II	V	I	VI

Dm7	G7	Em7	Am7	E7		E7	
II	V	III	VI	IIIx		IIIx	

Phrase Two (measures 9–16)

FMa7	G7	CMa7	Am7	Dm7	G7	Gm7	C7
IV	V	I	VI	II	V	Vm	Ix

FMa7		B7		Bb7		A7	
IV		VIIx		bVIIx		VIx	

Phrase Three (measures 17–24)

Dm7	G7	Em7	Am7	Dm7	G7	Em7 b5	A7
II	V	III	VI	II	V	III ø	VIx

Dm7		G7		C 6/9	Fm7	Em7	A7
II		V		I	IVm	III	VIx

When I teach tunes, especially Bill's, I always analyze the phrase structure first, then the key changes, if any (modulation principles), and then the use of secondary dominants, how they resolve and their duration. For example, the A7's at measures 16 and 20 resolve to the D minor chord, and we can infer that it is borrowed from the region or scale of D minor, which is only one flat removed from C Major, the scale or key of "Peri's Scope." In other words, the A7 suggests the key, the scale or "the region of" D minor, which is very closely related to the tonic key of C Major. I include in my thinking the relative major keys when discussing minor key relationships and relative minor keys when discussing major keys. This sounds confusing, I know, but as I analyze other compositions by Bill, you'll begin to grasp the principles I'm trying to explain. In fact, if you pick up the Theory of Harmony by Arnold Schoenberg, you will find out where Bill learned these principles and you'll be able to follow my explanations more intelligently.

Now go back and look at EX. 2, measures 8 & 9. The E7 at measure 8 resolves to an F Ma7 at measure 9. This E7 is borrowed from the scale of A minor, the relative minor of C Major, and it resolves deceptively, i.e. V to VI, or up a half step "as if" it were in the key of A minor. These are important considerations when studying this tune in terms of its horizontal or linear implications. We know that E7 is the dominant of A Major and A minor. But we probably wouldn't improvise on an A major scale at this point for two reasons: 1) the chords surrounding the E7 do not suggest a progression in A major, and 2) the resolution at measure 9 would have to be to an F# m7, the VI of A major, a deceptive resolution in the key of A major!

Let's get back to the voicing concepts. In EX. 2, measures 7 & 8, the voicing of the E7 is root, 7th, 10th (or 3rd), and in measure 9, the F Ma7 and G7 voicings are the same (R, 7th, 10th) because the root movement is stepwise, IIIx to IV to V. When progressions move by steps (IV-V or II-III, etc.), you can often move or lead the voices parallel. This makes for smoothness and clarity in the rendition of the tune. Any song will lend itself to this treatment. I call this the 3-note voicing concept and I learned it from Bill's model, "Peri's Scope."

In EX. 3, measure 14, the B7 is voiced root, 7th, 10th resolving to E7. The E7 here is the only voicing in our model that has no root. Or does it? I think Bill meant Bb7+5 at this point (last beat of measure 14). The B-natural in the bass was supposed to be a B-flat but was delayed to the next bar, measure 15, second beat. What do you think? If you accept my analysis, then the voicing to the Bb7 is parallel —R, 7th, 10th—and the resolution from Bb7 to the A7 in measure 16 is also parallel—R, 7th, 10th. Here's a look at these three chords in isolation (EX. 6). Play them!

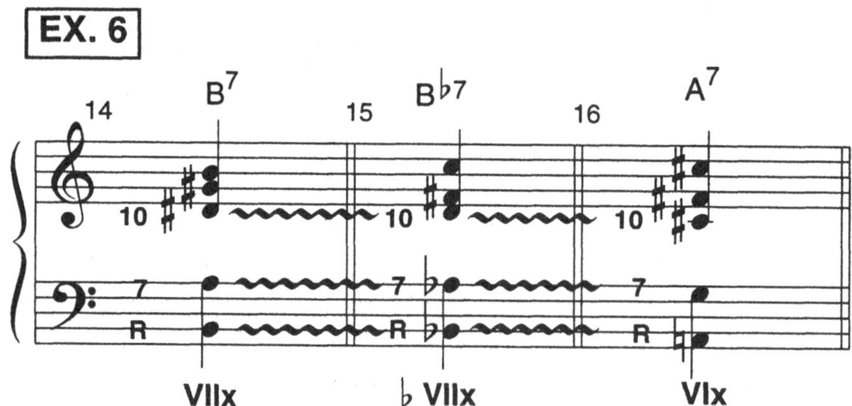

In EX. 7, measure 11, we see another variation in Bill's voicings, and a very simple one at that. He reduces the left hand voicing to two notes: R and 7th on the downbeat (D m7) and then R, 3rd on the third beat (G 7), while the melody in the right hand is harmonized in thirds. This gives us relief from the five part voicings in phrase one. In later performances of this piece, Bill changed measure 12 to Gm7, C7, suggesting that the middle phrase (phrase two, measures 9–16) can be heard as a modulation to the key of F Major, a very closely related key to C Major, one fifth down and one flat away from C Major.

These root-oriented 3-note voicing concepts formed the foundation of Bill's early style and permeated his later playing as you will see in my analysis of tunes like "B Minor Waltz."

In EX.8, measures 20 & 21, we observe more variety, the block chord voicing with melody on top and bottom. Bill knew his jazz piano history. I heard him play Boogie Woogie and Teddy Wilson styles in 1951. The block chord influences are from Milt Buckner and George Shearing.

And Bill even knew how to "sit" on the quarter note a la Lester Young at measure 19 to make it swing in the old style (EX. 9). Listen to Lester Young's solos on "Taxi War Dance" or "Blue Lester" with the Count Basie Orchestra for the quarter note swing "feel."

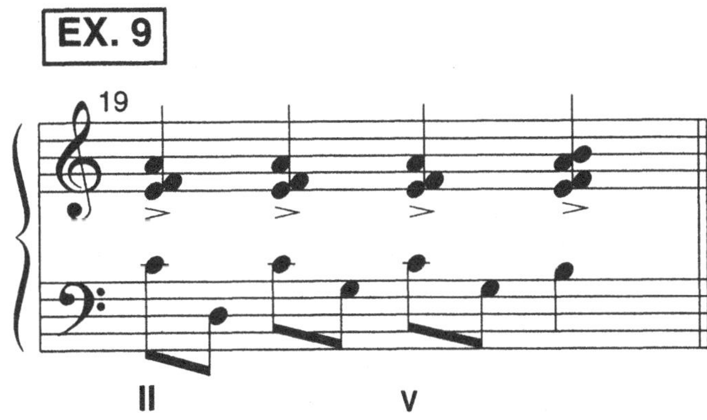

Notice the Boogie Woogie influence in the left hand of measure 19, the ultimate in sophistication. Bill truly "ingested" all the jazz styles of the past and they appear spontaneously in his writing and playing in extremely subtle ways. As a student of composition in the 50s, he "ingested" all the classical music of the past. In 1951 I heard him sightread, at the piano, the orchestral score to Stravinsky's "Rite of Spring." Of course, Bill's intuition is at play here; this is a welcome relief from all that rhythmic displacement, tension and syncopation in the previous phrase (EX. 10, measures 13–16.)

EX. 10 Phrase Two

I have made EX. 10 easier to learn. Let's look at my voicing arrangement (EX. 11) to explain what I mean. What I did was to notate in 6/8 what Bill notated as rhythmic displacement. I have subdivided the beat and created four measures in 6/8 out of Bill's three measures in 4/4.

EX. 11

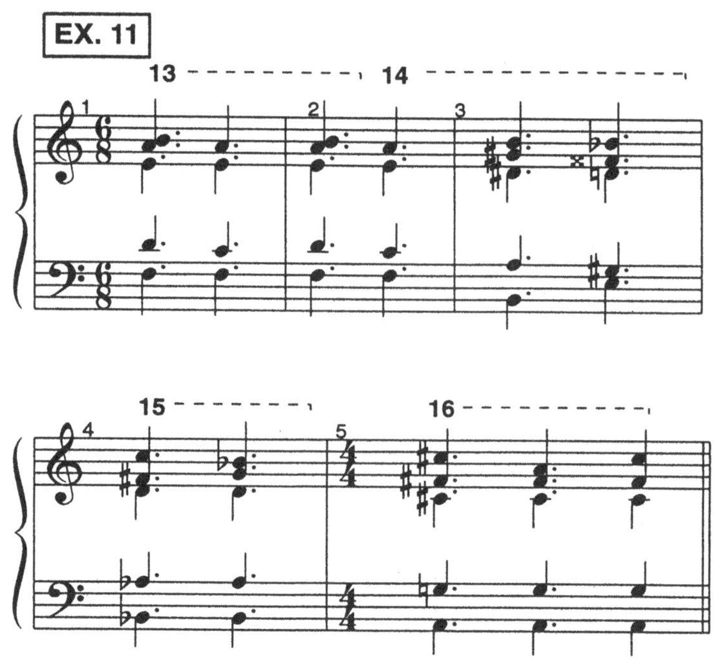

Bill may have conceived of this tune diatonically but his use of rhythmic displacement in phrase two makes the tune unmanageable for a beginner in improvisation unless he "evens out" those measures (see EX. 5, measures 13-16). Each phrase has wonderful variety of harmonic color (the addition of 9ths, 11ths, and 13ths), and unusual phrasing in the melody and in the piano voicings.

To conclude the article and at the same time offer you a recapitulation of the 3-note concept, here are two examples I use in teaching the Blues in F . In EX. 12, which you can analyze for yourself, you will see that I connect the chords by observing the voice leading rules explained earlier in this article. Analyze also EX. 13 and observe the addition of one color tone (9,11,13) above each of the 3-note voicings. (I make students write as many variations as possible using the color tones). Try singing "Billie's Bounce" melody while playing examples 12 & 13; or "Blue Monk," or have a friend play and improvise with you.

EX. 14 is the opening theme from the "Concertina for Strings and Piano," third movement, titled "Resurrection,"orchestrated brilliantly by Jack Six and premiered in December 1980, in Plainfield, New Jersey, Bill's hometown. The Concertina is dedicated to Bill's memory. In "Resurrection" you have a 3-note voicing arrangement of this very simple theme and yet it still sounds complete and satisfying. Incidentally, in this third movement, the piano soloist is called upon to invent variations on this theme, therefore the 3-note setting in the exposition of the movement creates a clear and solid statement of the theme. Bill was a master at arranging the opening chorus so as to set the mood for the listener in a positive and clear manner.

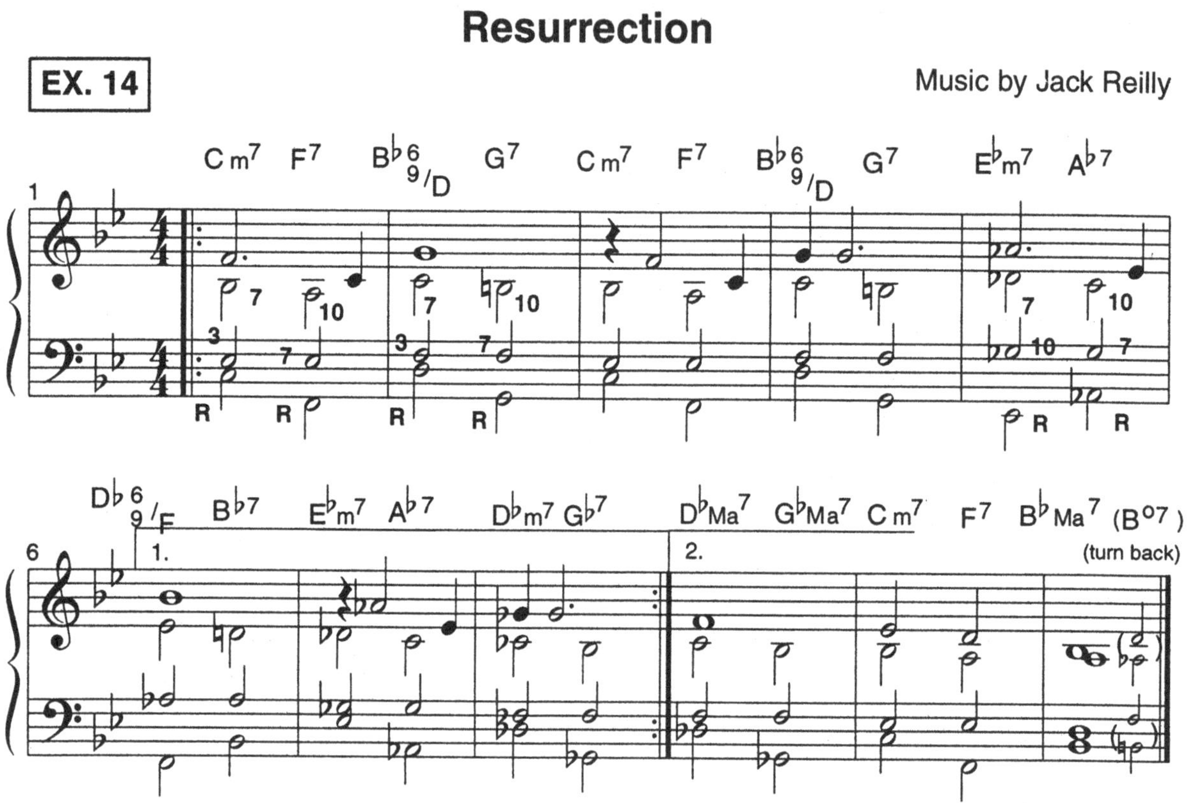

The final example (EX. 15) is an illustration of a more elaborate method of study for "Peri's Scope" and all of Bill's tunes, and in fact any tune, and that is to arrange the progression in 4, 5, 6, 7, or 8 parts in half-note chorale style. Bill would write out three or four examples like this and then practice them in all keys. For "Peri's Scope," I used the 3-note concept, adding a fourth part chosen by "ear," but notice that the soprano or top note I have chosen suggests or outlines the melody shown in the top staff. This is a good first step to get "inside" the tune. In the articles that follow, I will show many other procedures.

What I've learned from Bill is a precise method or discipline to the study and memorizing of the jazz repertoire. Here are the stages and the way he practiced.

STAGE ONE

A. Harmonize the tune using the 3-note voicing concept. Write it out on manuscript paper with melody above 3-notes, as I did in EX. 14, "Resurrection";

B. Practice the melody alone in all keys, gradually adding notes and changing the rhythm until you can improvise totally free of the melody;

C. Play the 3-note voicings without melody in all keys; sing the melody;

D. Transpose 3-note voicings with melody to all keys;

E. Add one color note to 3-note voicing (EX. 13) and transpose to all keys;

F. Write out the tune in question, as Bill did with "Peri's Scope." Play it in all keys, transposing exactly what you wrote in the original key.

STAGE TWO

A. Harmonize the tune in 4-part chorale style (EX. 15); transpose to all keys;
B. Then 5-part, 6-part, etc.

STAGE THREE

A. Explore the tune using only strict 4-part classical voicings of seventh chords (no color tones) in all inversions. This final stage is very demanding because the goal is to be able to improvise on the voicings. Bill's solo on "Nardis" (Paris Concert—ELEKTRA MUSICIAN) is an example of what can develop by practicing all three stages.

In the next article, I return to "Peri's Scope," but only to the melody line. I thoroughly analyze its motific and phrase structure to show you how Bill has composed such a tightly knit theme that if you change one note, or one rhythm, you destroy the entire piece! I also introduce to you the idea or concept of the "basic shape." It's a concept of form, meaning that an entire composition, and in Bill's case , an entire improvisation, develops and evolves from the "basic shape."

Later in the book, I tackle "Time Remembered." This gives me the opportunity to explore 7-part voicings of major and minor thirteenths, since this forms the basis of the harmonic structure of "Time Remembered." For me, "Time Remembered" is an amazing creation not only for its finely crafted melody but because Bill does not use any dominant 7th chords in the whole piece. As part of my analysis, I show you that the voicings Bill employs in this arrangement are based on four different ways of voicing seventh chords that he learned from his study of classical theory and from his playing of the classical piano literature. In terms of voicing principles, "Time Remembered" builds on those of "Peri's Scope" very logically, but in terms of piano technique, it is a much more difficult piece and even a bit awkward to play. For the latter reason, I've decided to give you many fingerings which should help you play it in a more legato style. They are advanced fingerings which have taken me eight months to a year to solidify. Bill Evans, you're worth it!

PERI'S SCOPE

THEMATIC ANALYSIS

In this article, I will analyze the thematic material of Bill's tune, "Peri's Scope." My purpose will be to gain insight into the principles of good melody writing and, in Bill's case, to get inside the creative mind of a genius as that mind organized, developed and evolved his compositions by following the dictates of what Schoenberg calls the "BASIC SHAPE," the seed thought, the germ or idea that generates the entire piece. Because I use in these articles a specific vocabulary when I discuss Bill's thematic material, I think it best to define these terms before I begin the analysis.

MOTIF—an interval, harmony, and/or rhythm combining to produce memorable shapes or patterns; a motif appears continually throughout a piece; it is repeated. Repetition alone often gives rise to monotony, and monotony can only be overcome by variation.

VARIATION—a change in some of the less important features of the motif and the preservations of some of the more important ones.

FIGURE—a smaller rhythmic and/or melodic feature of the motif that is repeated throughout the piece. A dotted quarter followed by an eighth note is a rhythmic figure Bill uses continually in "Peri's Scope."

DIRECTIONAL TONES—the range and contour (high and low points) of the theme; the main pitches that outline the theme.

INVERSION—an ascending pattern that later descends, and vice versa.

AUGMENTATION—an increased time value according to a ratio (three eighth notes become triplets, etc.).

DIMINUTION—a decreased time value according to a ratio (eighth notes become sixteenth notes).

RETROGRADE—the theme or motif played, or repeated backwards.

BASIC SHAPE—usually the first idea which generates the whole piece.

PHRASE—a complete musical thought, like a sentence in English (in this piece, 8 measures).

Let's look at EX. 1A to 1C (measures 1 - 2). This is the BASIC SHAPE. The melodic figures are one lonely eighth note, a "g" on the first beat, rhythmic space or silence for one and one-half beats, a descending four note scale pattern, "g" to "d," and an ascending interval leap of a perfect fourth, "d" to "g." The DIRECTIONAL TONES and range are easy to calculate, "g" down to "d," back up to "g." The range is a perfect fourth. These are the memorable melodic features of Motif 1. But it's the rhythmic, syncopated figures (EX. 1E) which give Motif 1 its uniqueness and announce that "Peri's Scope" is a jazz composition! I have found six different ways to break down Motif 1 into FIGURES. Can you find more?

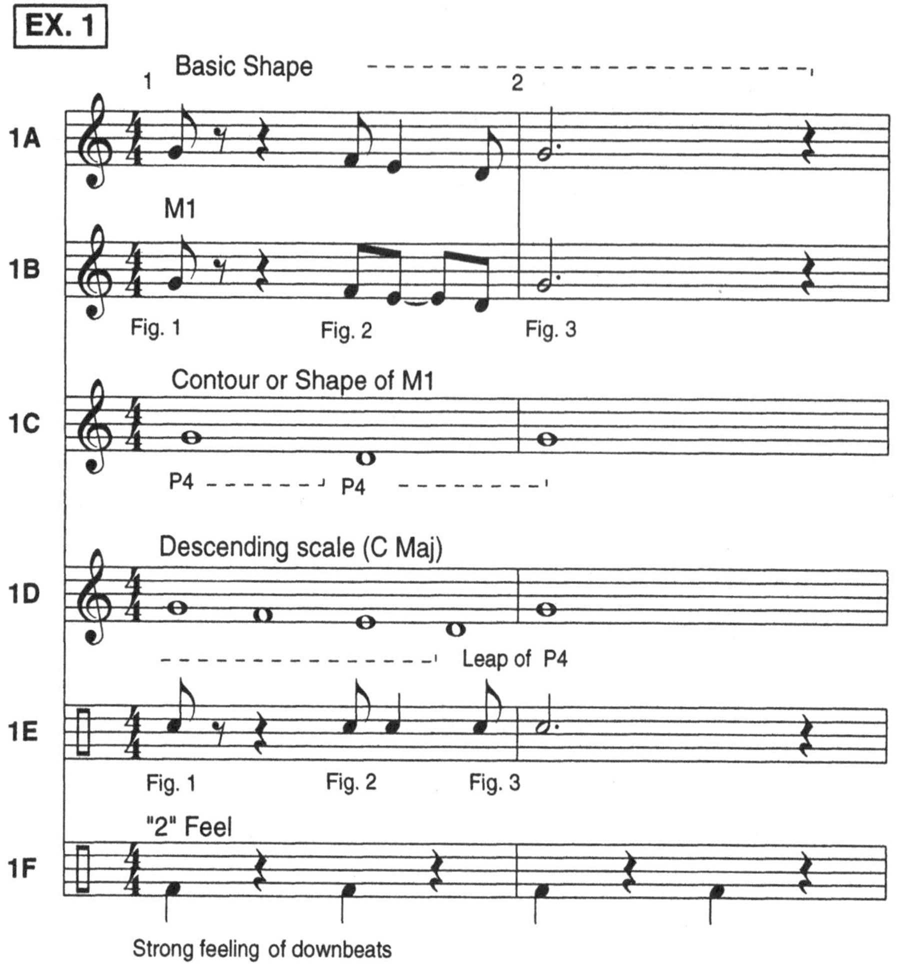

Motif 2 is a development and repetition of the melodic and rhythmic figures of Motif 1. Compare EX. 2A with my analysis in EX. 2C. Bill's VARIATION of the four note scale pattern results in a broken scale pattern in thirds. The interval leap of a perfect fourth he expands to a perfect fifth; that is, he leaped from "d" to "a." The syncopation he shifts to the "and-of" 4, measure 3, and again on the "and-of" 3, measure 4. This last syncopated note of motif 2 is "g," the same pitch that begins "Peri's Scope"! And it's also an eighth note! The rhythmic silence or space in measure 4 lasts for two beats, the same amount of rhythmic space that separates Motif 1 from Motif 2. Are these relationships accidental? I don't think so. There is an inner "logician" at work here, the mind of the composer. Oh, yes, the range of Motif 2 is one octave.

Then in measure 5, Bill offers another VARIATION in the rhythmic pattern of measure three by introducing sixteenth notes and a quarter-note triplet for the first time (EX. 3A). His ear immediately picks up on the sixteenth notes, so we get more of them in the very next measure! (EX. 3B).

With all of this incredible melodic and rhythmic variation so far (measures 1–6), the DIRECTIONAL TONES hint at monotony. Why? They all hover around the pitch "g"! What does Mr. Evans do? He lets the "composer" step in, and in measure 7 he writes not one, but two "g-sharps," the first chromatic note of the piece (EX. 4). How does he rhythmically treat these "g-sharps"? By holding the first one for one and one-half beats and syncopating the second one. This is breathtaking. It is in this measure that Bill reveals to us that he is inwardly singing. How does he reveal this? By following the "g#s" with six beats of rhythmic space: silence! Now he is able to make a new breath. And that is precisely how we can identify the end of one phrase and the beginning of another. Measures 1- 8 comprise phrase one; measures 9–16, phrase two; measures 17–24, phrase three.

The syncopated FIGURE in measure 7 is not unique. It reappears in measures 13 -16, the second part of phrase two, where Bill the composer fully exploits it (EX. 5A), as the climax or high point of "Peri's Scope." It is the dotted quarter note, however, that is secretly exploited by alternate syncopation, i.e. every other quarter note is placed on the "and" of the beat. To make this clear in my analysis, I have rewritten these FIGURES in 6/8 meter (EX. 5B). Because of this rhythmic complexity, the inner "logician" tells Bill to narrow the range. Now he has the opportunity to create melodic FIGURES on the intervals of a Major 2nd, minor 2nd, minor 3rd, and Major 3rd (EX. 5C).

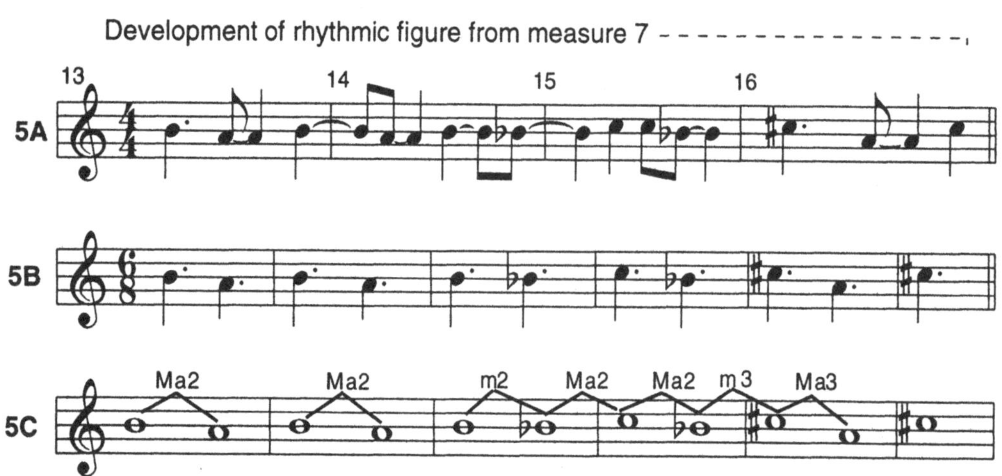

See Ex. 6 and 7 for further analyses of Motifs 1 and 2.

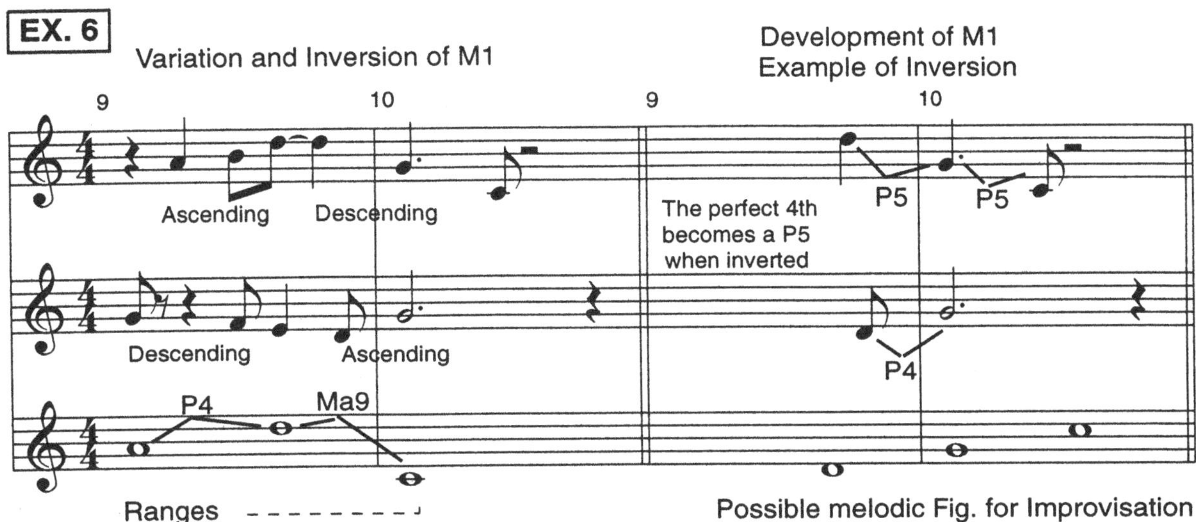

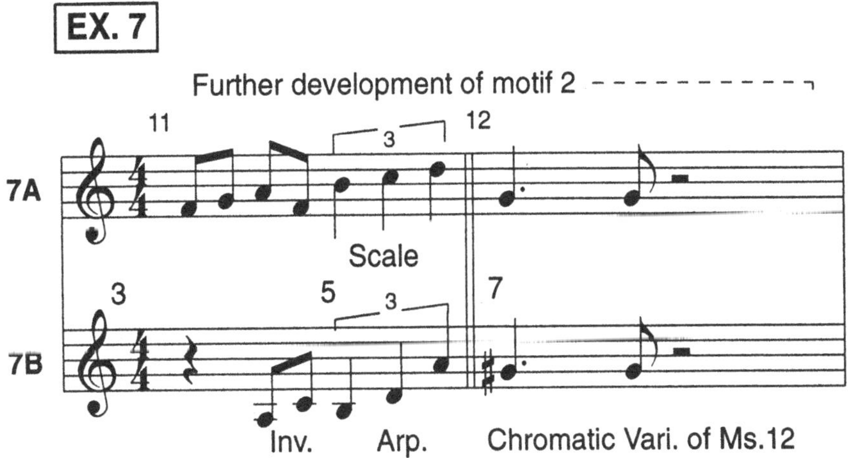

"TIME REMEMBERED"
HARMONIC ANALYSIS

"Time Remembered" must have emerged from very deep within the musical mind of Bill Evans or, as he might have put it, from the "universal mind." It is a composition that harmonically pays homage to the Modal period in music history, the sixteenth century that gave birth to Palestrina, Byrd, Caccini, Morley, Monteverdi, Frescobaldi, and Schutz. The harmonies and progressions of "Time Remembered" suggest four modes or scales that formed the basis of many of the works of that period: the Dorian, Phrygian, Lydian, and Aeolian. The Bach chorales of the seventeenth century mark the transition from Modality to Tonality (major/minor system). We then had to wait three hundred years for a reincarnation of the modes in the compositions of Debussy and Ravel. Bill knew these two Impressionistic masters inside and out, and in "Time Remembered," he has compressed within 26 measures four hundred years of musical evolution from Modality to Tonality to Impressionism.

The unique thing about "Time Remembered" is the inconspicuous absence of the dominant 7th chord and its derivatives, the half-diminished and the full-diminished. When Bill had eliminated these, he was left with only major and minor chords. For this reason, the piece sounds impressionistic and modal. He has met the challenge of writing a tune with only two harmonic qualities by introducing unusual root movements and by exploiting the use of the upper partials (9, 11, 13) in the melody. Let's look at EX. 1 in which I have reduced the original to four parts. The root is always in the bass. The 3rd, 5th, and 7th, however, are voiced in a variety of ways, according to the new voicing categories that I will explain shortly.

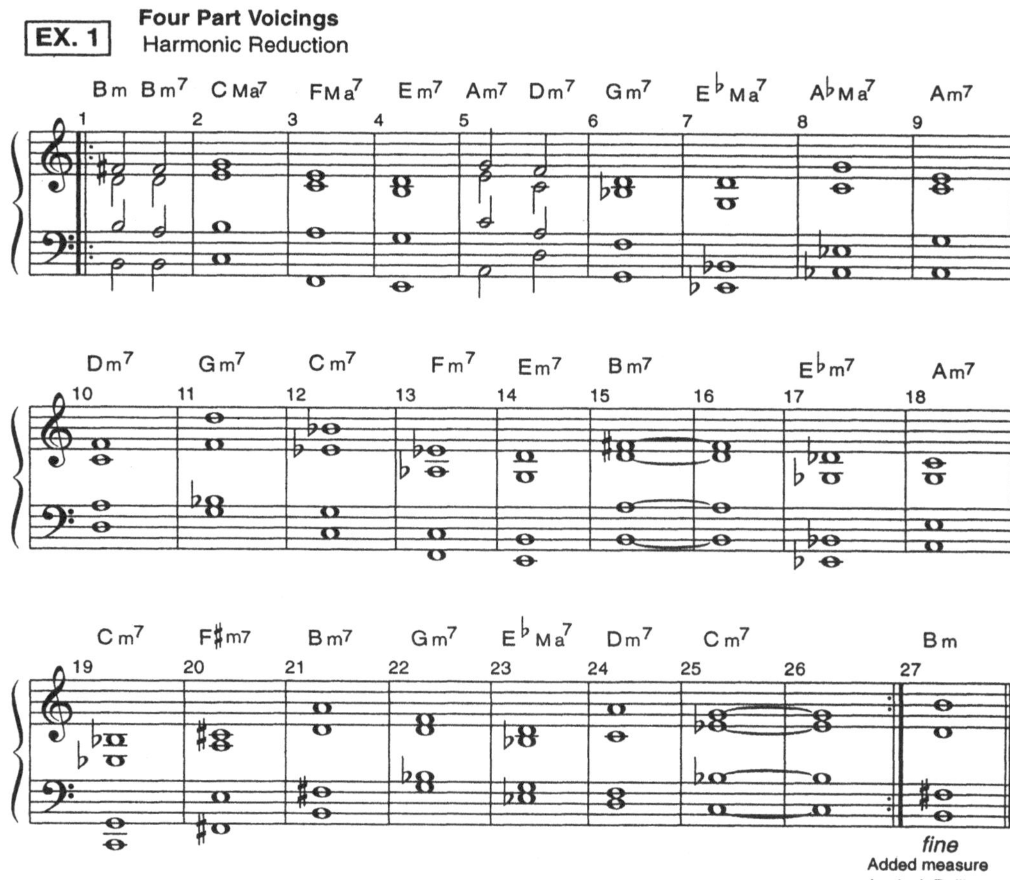

The original Bill Evans score of "Time Remembered" (EX. 2) is one of Bill's most complex contrapuntal scores. It's equal in difficulty to Bach's *Five-Part Fugue in C-sharp* from Book One of the Well-Tempered Clavier. To help you to achieve a better legato, I have written a set of fingerings. Also, you might have a look at the Fugue. It's a good preparatory piece for "Time Remembered."

Now look at EX. 1 and listen for the harmonic qualities of Ma7 or m7; observe the voicings; feel them in your hands. Now visualize the 5th omitted. What's left? The root, 3rd, and 7th, of course: the three-note concept. By adding the 5th to all the chords in "Time Remembered," Bill has quadrupled the voicing possibilities. He has also created five new voicing categories. The voicings in measures 1, 2, 6, 9, 15, 25, 26, and 29, I call category "A": the root, 7th, 3rd, and 5th. In measures 5 (third beat only), 10 and 18, the voicing is root, 5th, 7th, and 3rd. Let's call this category "B." In measures 7, 8, 12, 13, 14, 17, 19, and 21, Bill voices the chords root, 5th, 3rd, and 7th. We'll name these the "C" voicings. Next we read root, 3rd, 7th, and 5th in measures 11 and 24. This will be the "D" voicing category. Lastly, in measures 3, 4, 5 (first beat only), 22, and 23, Bill uses block voicings. This makes up our fifth category, the "E" voicings.

To make it easier to follow this analysis, I have rewritten and organized EX. 1 by voicing categories. Refer now to EX. 3A, 3B, 3C, 3D, and 3E (bar numbers under EX. 3A–3E indicate which measure(s) contains the voicing category. For example, bars 1 & 15 are examples of "A" voicings, etc.). I have also written out all inversions appropriate to each voicing category. Exhaust all possibilities! That's my motto. Bill did. He spent hours and hours practicing these fundamental four-part voicings, in every category, in root position and all inversions, and in all keys, until they were "second nature." Nobody else since Art Tatum has had such an enormous voicing vocabulary "in the fingers." And Bill has surpassed Tatum in this department owing to his broader knowledge of classical music, especially the music of Debussy, Ravel, and Stravinsky.

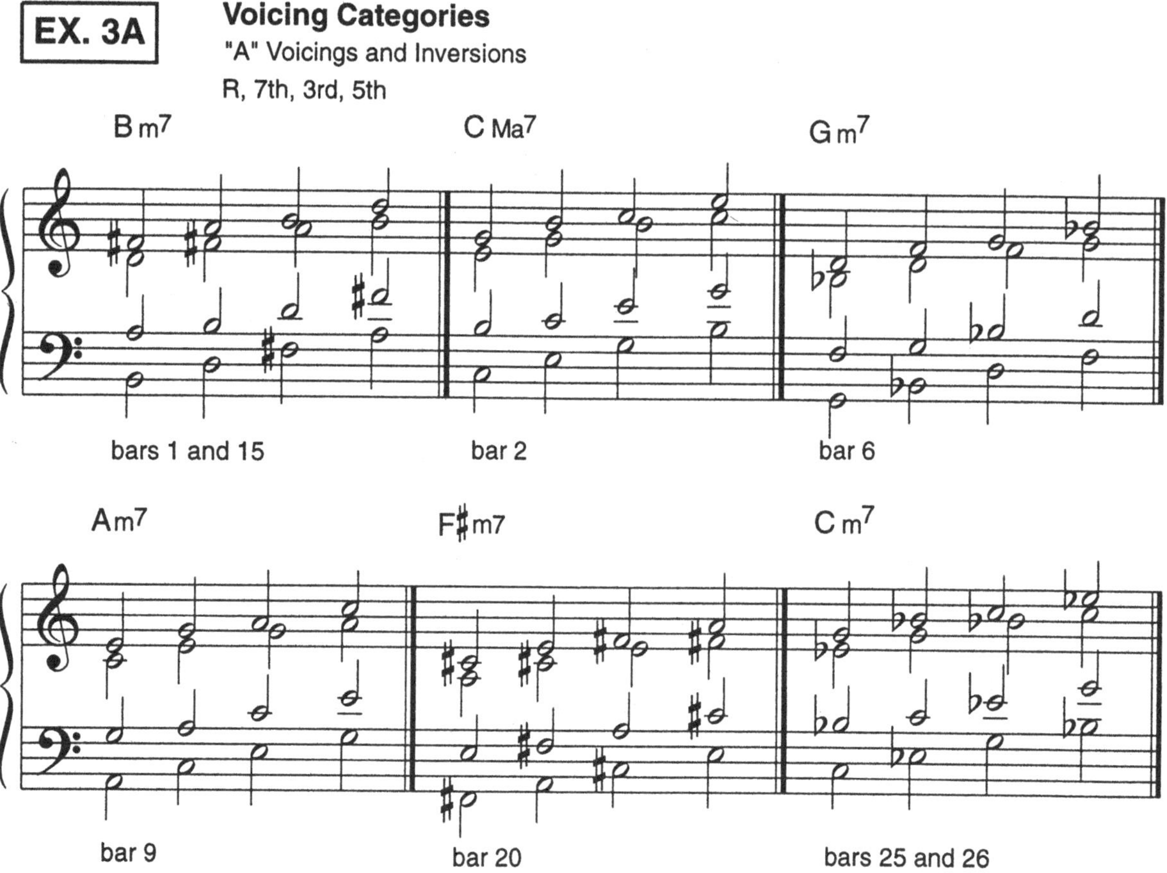

EX. 3B "B" Voicings and Inversions
R, 5th, 7th, 3rd

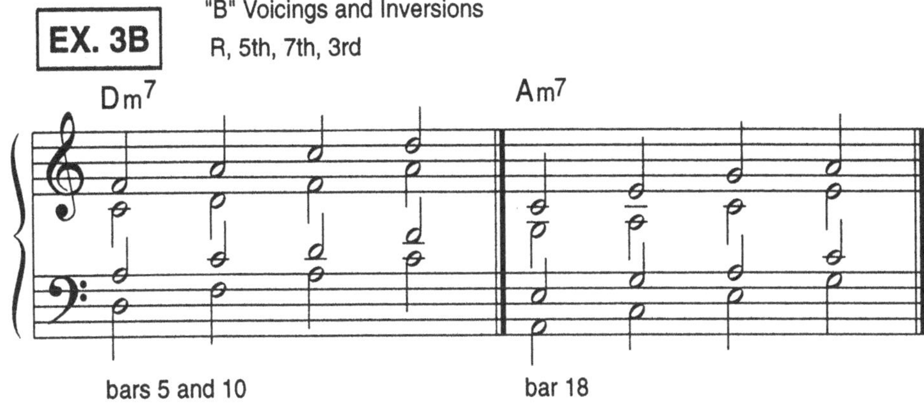

EX. 3C "C" Voicings and Inversions
R, 5th, 3rd, 7th

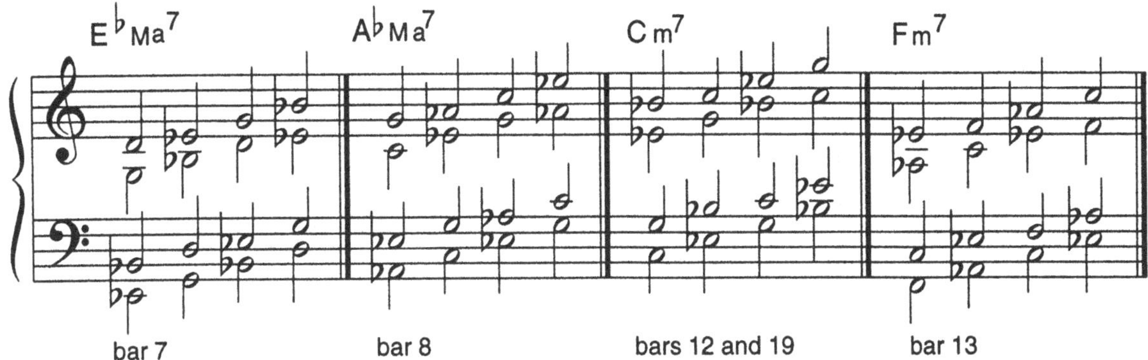

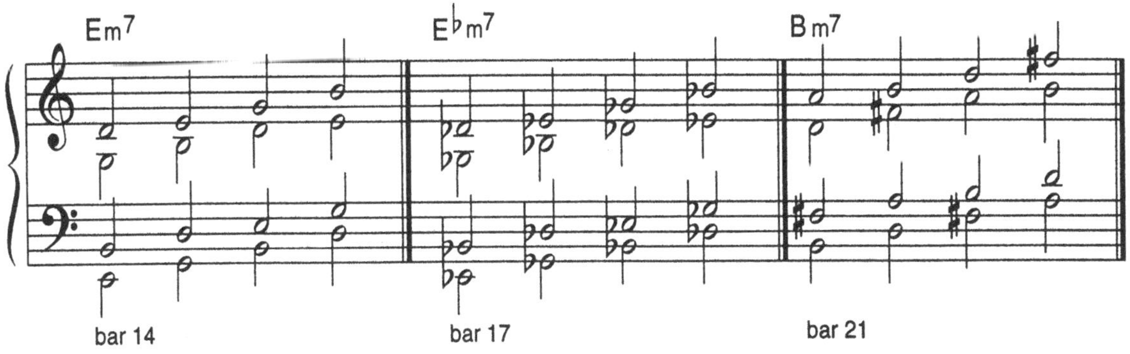

EX. 3D "D" Voicings and Inversions
R, 3rd, 7th, 5th

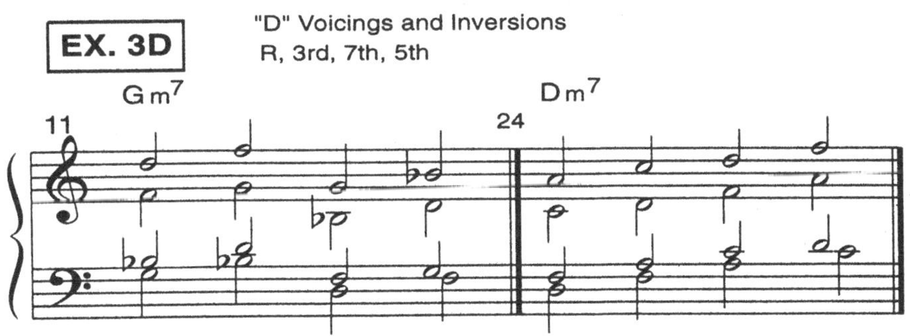

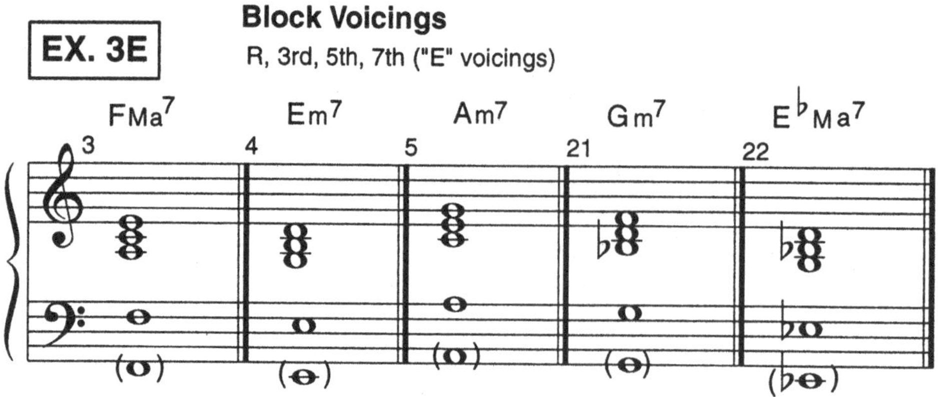

When I first met Bill Evans in 1951, I witnessed his reading, at the piano, the orchestral score to Stravinsky's *The Rite of Spring*, reducing the parts to fit his hands. He didn't miss a note! Since then, his sight-reading ability has become legendary. That skill can only be developed by spending hours at your instrument reading something new every minute. But in Bill's case, he sight-read for knowledge alone.

Now I will analyze in detail measures 7 and 8 from the original score. See EX. 4. Bill has written an Eb Ma13th resolving up a fourth to Ab Ma13th. Can you see the basic four-part seventh chord voicings and categories hidden in these seven-part chords? Not yet? Then look at EX. 4A.

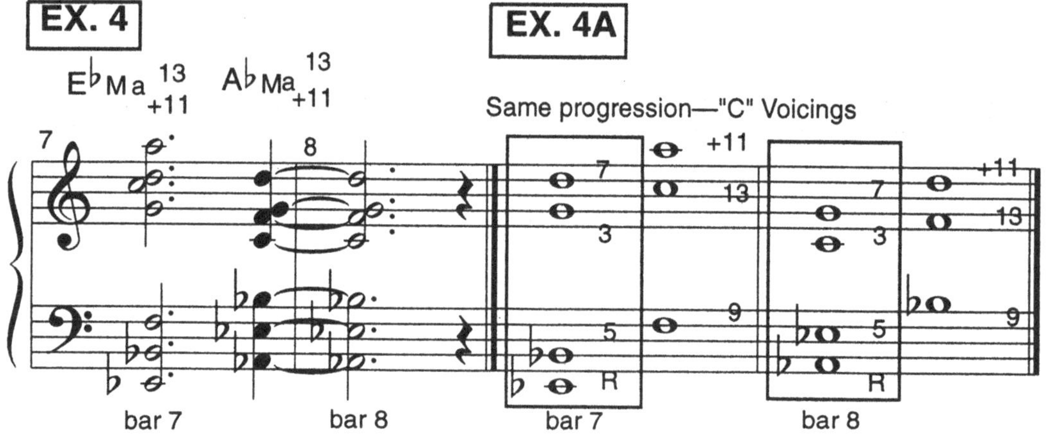

Here I have isolated the basic four parts from the upper partials. (This is what the harmonic reduction in EX. 1 is all about). It is now clear that both chords belong to the "C" voicing category (See EX. 3C). Separated in EX. 4A, the upper partials now look like major triads. But they also belong to the Eb and Ab Ma7 chords as the 9th, +11th, and 13th. Here's a simple rule to follow: by visualizing major triads superimposed one whole step above Ma7ths, you will learn to play seven-part Ma13th chords quickly. Such practice is also the first step toward thinking in polytonal relationships.

Now look at EX. 5, 5A, and 5B. In these examples, I have placed the upper partials of the EbMa13th with the inversions. Further experimentation will reveal other possibilities. Then you can do what Bill did: at the piano transpose your experiments to all keys until they are "in the fingers."

EX. 5 EX. 5A EX. 5B

E♭ Ma 9 +11 /G E♭ Ma 9 +11 13 /B♭ E♭ Ma 9 +11 13 /D E♭ Ma 9 +11 13

In EX. 6 and 6A, my analysis of measure 6 from Bill's original score (see EX. 2) follows the same procedure as in EX. 4 through 5B. Only this time I have chosen the minor chord quality, which in this measure is a Gm13th.

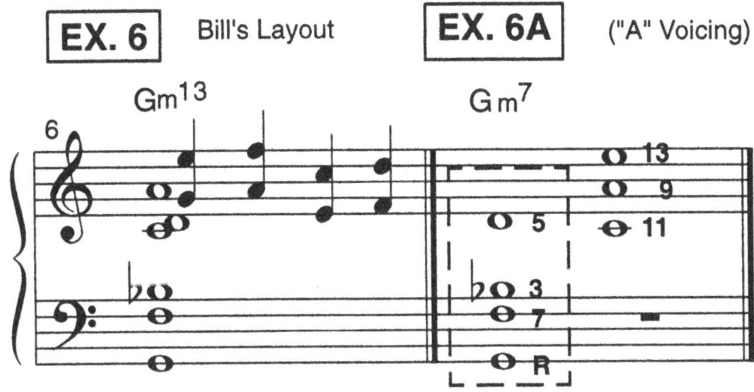

Now examine EX. 7 for the use of the upper partials with the inversions of the Gm13th.

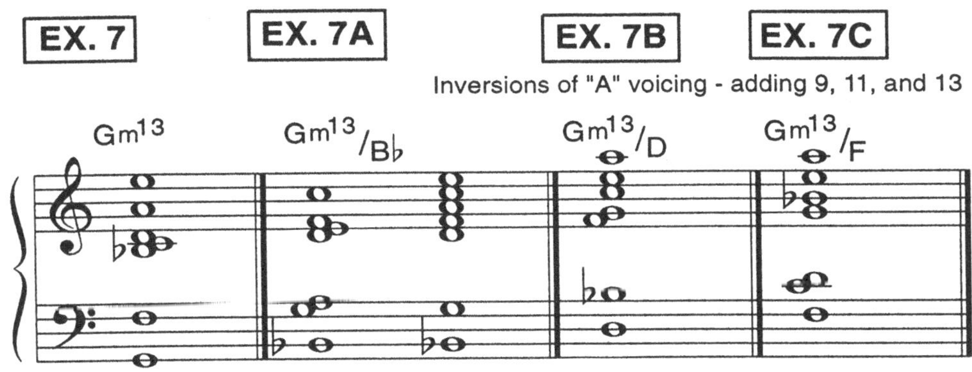

(Divide the hands, or roll chords from bottom to top)

Analyze each measure of Bill's score in a similar manner and you'll complete the harmonic picture of "Time Remembered." By a careful study of all the chord categories in this article, you will now have a method by which to work out the analysis of all Bill's original scores on your own. Continue to experiment with all the chord categories from EX. 3A through 3E by placing the 9th, +11th, and 13th within the voicing of the basic four-part 7th chords that I have written out for you in these examples.

In the final example (EX. 8), I have written a seven-part voicing arrangement of "Time Remembered" based on all the principles discussed above and in the "Peri's Scope" articles. Examine each measure and try to separate the basic four-part voicing by writing it next to my seven-part realization. Analyze the chord voicing category. I have worked out the first three measures for you (EX. 8, measures 1–3).

EX. 8
Seven-Part Voicings
(Major and minor 13ths)
"C" voicing
"B" voicing
inversion of "B" voicing
continue . . .

TIME REMEMBERED
MODAL ANALYSIS

This analysis totally ignores the harmonic progression composed by Bill, in order to observe the theme as a complete entity; one that doesn't need harmony to prove its existence.

In the Modal period (pre-Bach), polyphony reigned supreme; harmony was accidental and therefore not a factor in determining the form or length of a composition. The theoretical basis derived from this period was the MODES or scales: Ionian, Dorian, Phrygian, Lydian, MixoLydian, Aeolian, and Locrian, all beginning on the pitch "c." After Bach, the modes disappeared, or rather, were swallowed up, allowing for a synthesis which gave birth to the major/minor system and a theory of harmony based on 12 major and 12 minor scales (called scales to differentiate between the pre-Bach Modal period and the Tonal post-Bach era). This tonal period lasted roughly 300 years before a new and higher synthesis—Atonality—came into being.

When a synthesis is reached, it always inherits the previous period. Inherent in the Tonal system is the Modal system; inherent in the Atonal system are both the Modal and the Tonal systems. Bill Evans was born with this awareness, and through his study of the Schoenberg harmony, counterpoint, and compositional books, he created his wonderfully rich compositions, full of the past and present and achieving a new synthesis: the conscious merging of classical music with jazz.

There is a term coined by Gunther Schuller: "Third Stream Music." It means the synthesis of two streams, classical and jazz, to produce a third stream. Bill Evans' compositions are Third Stream, and the following analysis of "Time Remembered" is an attempt to prove that statement true.

Here are eight examples that break down the theme into eight phrases (the measure lengths are altered slightly for Part 1). Each example show how the theme expresses a mode based on the gravity caused by the succession of tones in each phrase. The clue lies in the Directional Tones in each phrase. In EX. 1A, our ear retains (remembers) the opening "f#" at the arrival of the last note "b," and identifies these pitches as the dominant or 5th note (f#) and tonic (1st note) of the B Aeolian mode.

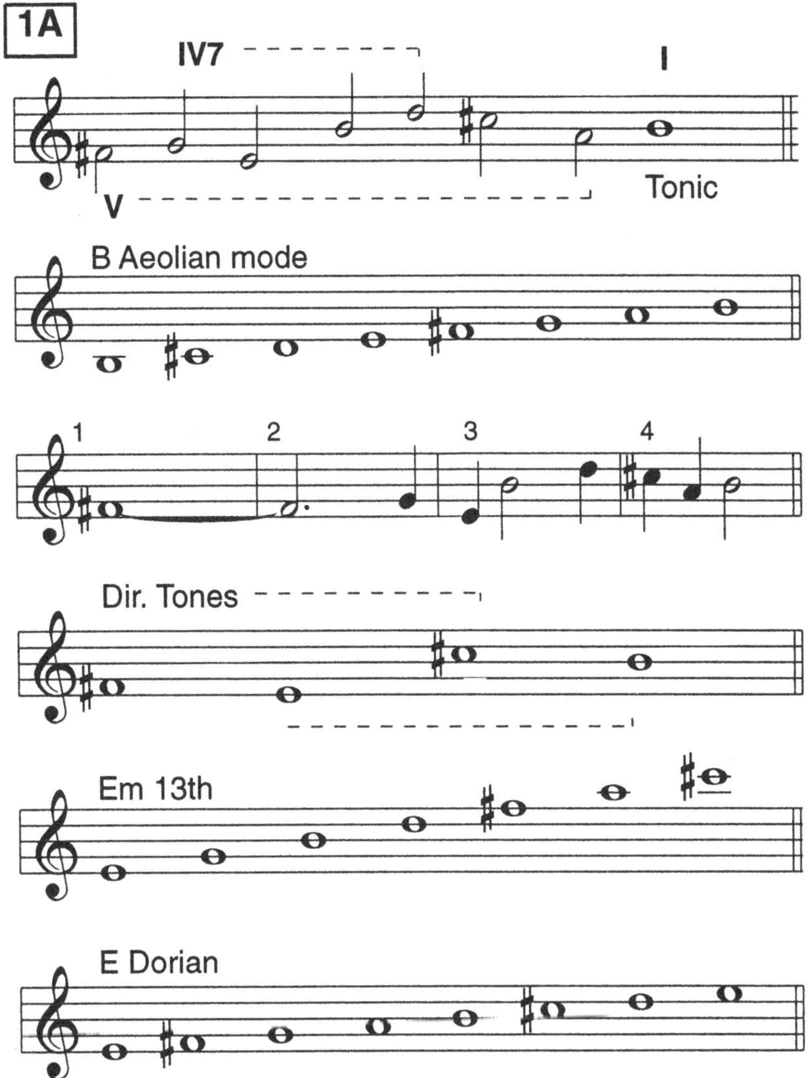

The rest of the pitches in this phrase support this conclusion. "C#" is the super-tonic note, "a" is the leading tone, "e" the sub-dominant, etc. The high point on the pitch "d" links up with the "f#" and "b" to form a tonic B minor triad, but I must not use that to support my conclusion, since I stated above that this analysis is linear (horizontal) and not chordal (vertical)!

Our ear does, however, group (link) tones to form chords because it's almost impossible to forget our 20th century inheritance: harmony! I have therefore included an analysis of what our 20th century ear picks up chord-wise in each example. Looking at EX. 1A again, you'll see that my ear groups these pitches vertically to form a V7, IV7 & I chord (F#m7, Em7 & Bm triad respectively). The modes are very slippery and our ear could very easily shift the tonic to the pitch "e," giving us an E Dorian mode. This is obvious because both the B Aeolian and E Dorian contain the same pitches. In the latter instance, my ear picked up the Directional Tone "e" (low point, and linked it with the "b" in measure 4, plus the opening "f#," pulling me gravitationally to the "e" as a tonic note).

In each of the following examples, you must sing (and/or play) the phrase as written; then sing the analytical sections above and below; then sing the modes; then repeat and repeat until your ear gravitates toward the tonic of each mode. It is entirely within the realm of probability that you will arrive at other modal conclusions, but remember, it is the Directional Tones—the high and low point in each phrase—that will support my conclusion. I'll stand firmly on all of them! Ultimately, it should be child's play when you finally sit down with this wonderful composition, "Time Remembered."

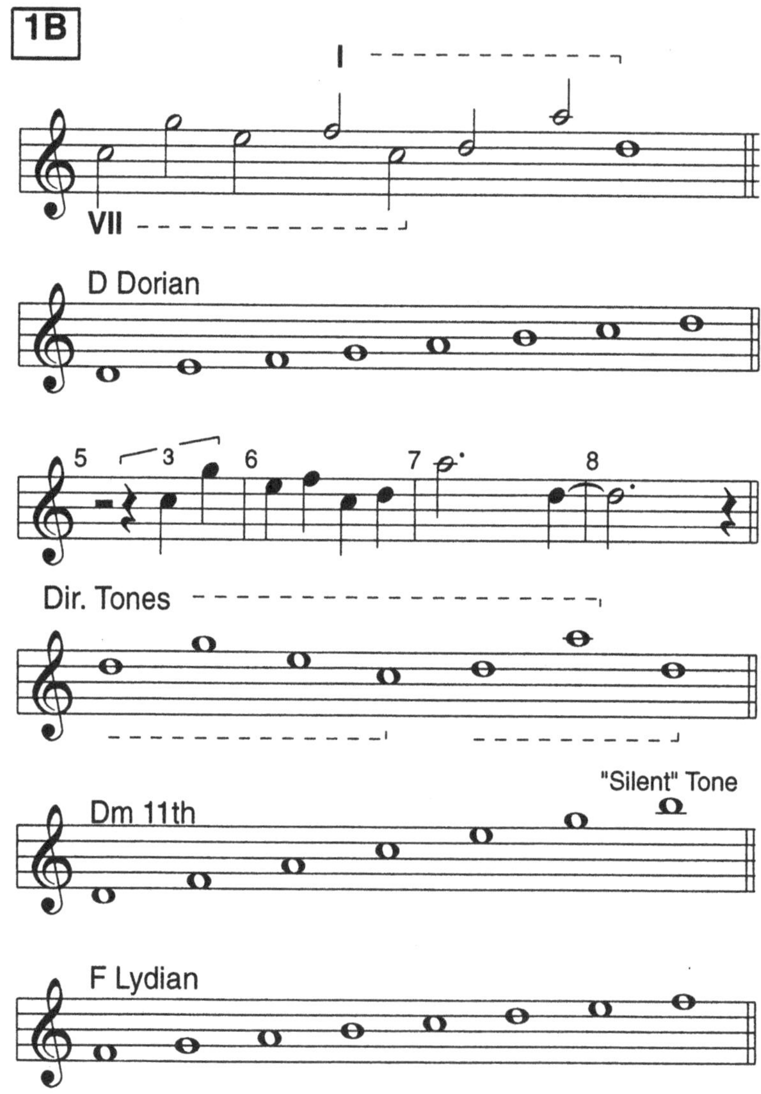

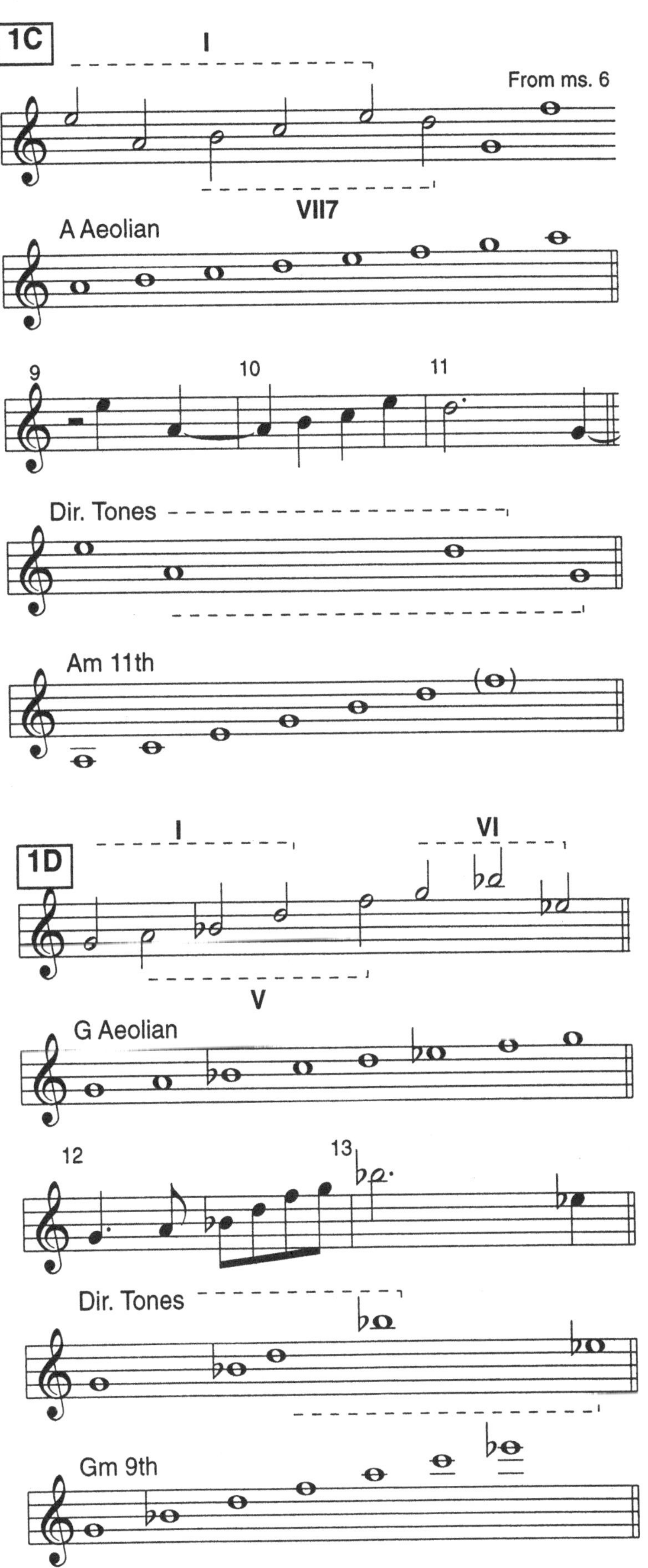
1C
I
From ms. 6
VII7
A Aeolian
9
10
11
Dir. Tones
Am 11th
I
VI
1D
V
G Aeolian
12
13
Dir. Tones
Gm 9th

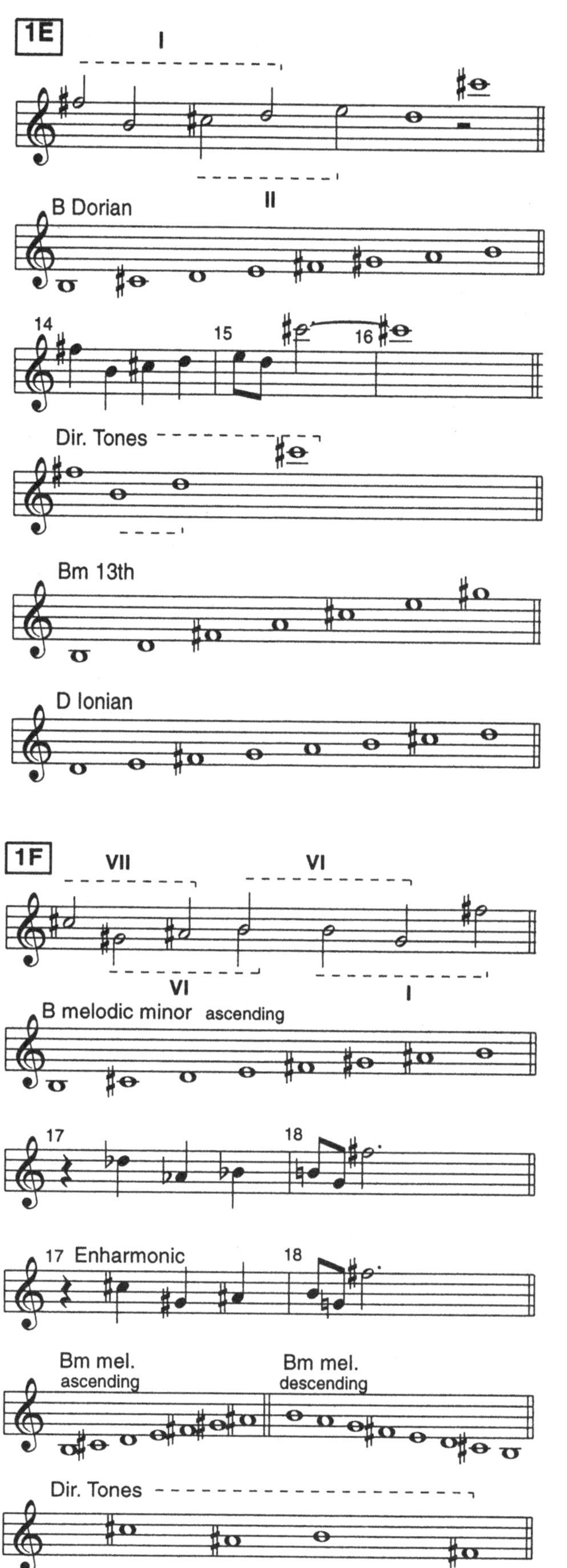
1E
I
II
B Dorian
14
15
16
Dir. Tones
Bm 13th
D Ionian
1F
VII
VI
VI
I
B melodic minor ascending
17
18
17 Enharmonic
18
Bm mel. ascending
Bm mel. descending
Dir. Tones

1G
19
20
21
G♯ mel.
ascending
descending
Dir. Tones

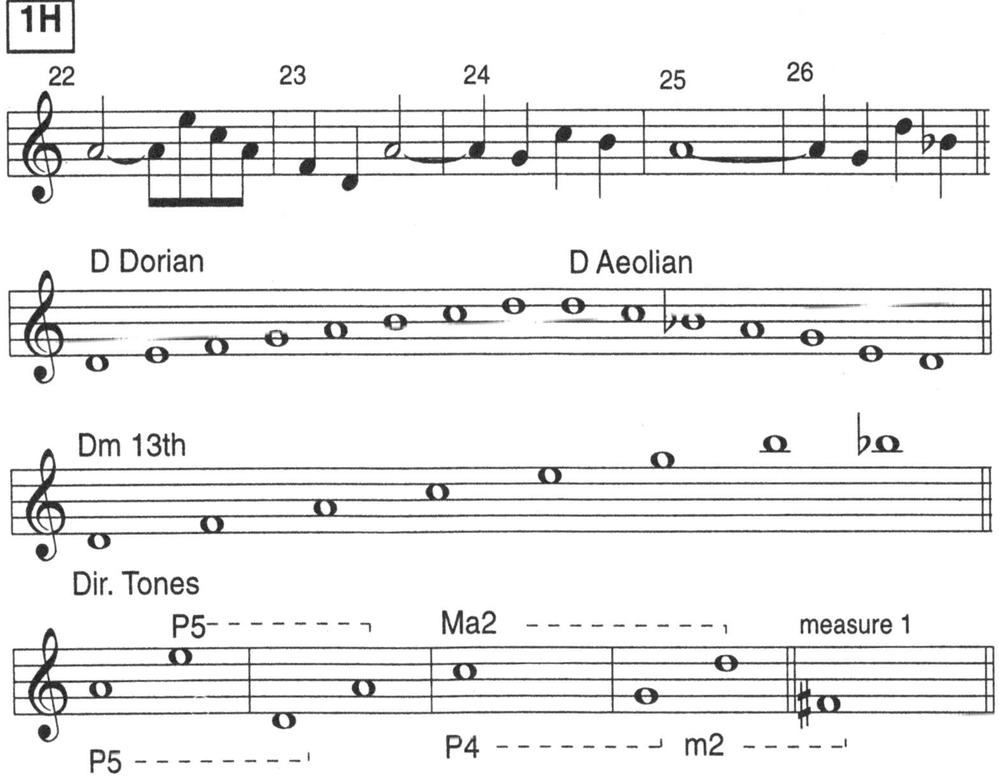
1H
22
23
24
25
26
D Dorian
D Aeolian
Dm 13th
Dir. Tones
P5
Ma2
measure 1
P5
P4
m2

TIME REMEMBERED
INTERVALLIC ANALYSIS

There are four ways to analyze themes:

1. **INTERVALLICALLY**—by measuring the theme note by note and naming the distance in pitch, we arrive at each interval that is formed in the unfolding of the thematic material. In so doing, it is hoped to find an underlying pattern, or specific intervals that give the theme its expressive power and uniqueness; we then look for the Directional Tones (the high and low point of each phrase). These reveal other patterns and characteristics that make up the "shape" of the theme.

2. **MODALLY**—by re-grouping the tones of each phrase, we form a scale or scales (modes).

3. **HARMONICALLY**—by relating the tones to the harmony, we again look for significant melodic patterns and color.

4. **MOTIFICALLY**—by breaking down the phrases into smaller units called motifs (melodic cells), and then the motifs to smaller units called figures (molecules).

Since this article addresses intervallic relationships, see EX. 1A through 1H below for the intervallic breakdown of the theme (26 measures, 8 phrases with subdivisions).

Observe that in phrase one, the theme consists of intervals of minor and major 2nds, dividing the phrase in half by a perfect 5th. A unique pattern emerges here; the first three notes—"f#," "g," and "e"—and the 5th, 6th and 7th notes—"d," "c#," and "a"—are made up of similar intervals, seconds and thirds, with the pitch "b" separating them and ending the phrase (see brackets and boxes). Another observation to make is that the phrase begins with an interval of a minor 2nd but ends with a major 2nd, a very subtle dramatic effect.

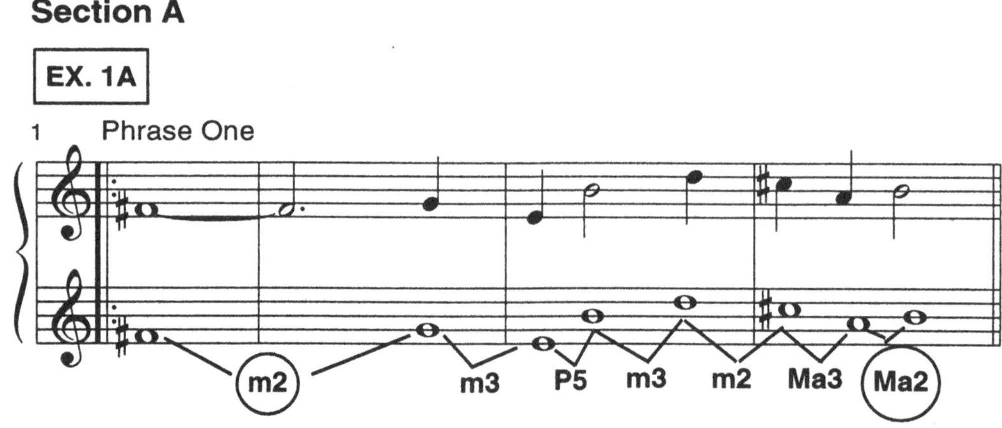

Here Bill begins with a perfect 5th and ends with a perfect 5th, creating a feeling of calm; more 2nds, 3rds and, for the first time, a perfect 4th, subdividing the phrase in half.

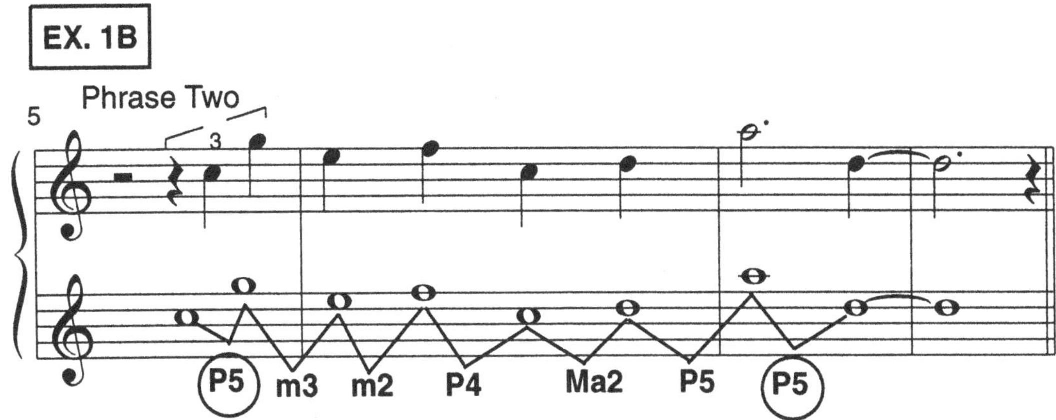

Now for the first time we have a three-measure phrase (another four-measure phrase here would be monotonous). Perfect 5ths begin and end the phrase, with only 2nds and 3rds between. A keen observer would suggest that this phrase subdivides in 3's (1 + 1 + 1); measure 9 begins with a descending perfect 5th ("e" to "a") and measure 11 ends with another descending perfect 5th but this time "d" to "g"!! Measure 10 is the surprise: "b" to "c" to "e," the exact inversion of our 3-note pattern in the first phrase ("d" to "c#" to "a").

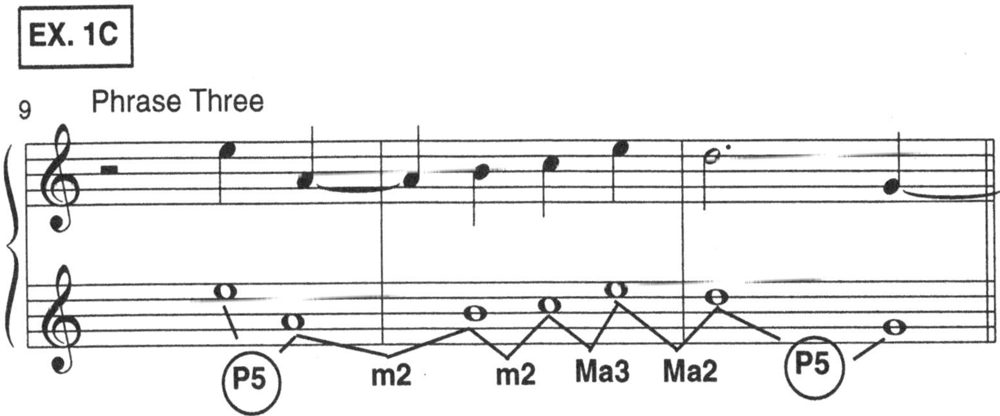

In phrase four, Section A comes to a half cadence on the pitch "c#," the ninth of the B minor chord, the same chord that began the piece. We encounter a five-measure phrase, a subtle extension of the four-measure phrases one and two. Bill achieves this by tying over the "c#" for one full measure. This was a stroke of genius because a lesser talent would not have tied over the "c#" at measure 16 and no one would have noticed the difference. If you don't believe me, try playing the theme from measures 1–15, skip measure 16, and continue to measures 17–26. Now play it again adding measure 16. What do you feel? Right! The need for SPACE; a chance to BREATHE, and measure 16 is the perfect place. We also meet for the first time at measure 15 an interval of a major 7th, a very passionate interval, full of energy and tension; therefore, the necessity to halt, stop, breathe. How? Tie over the "c#" for one full measure.

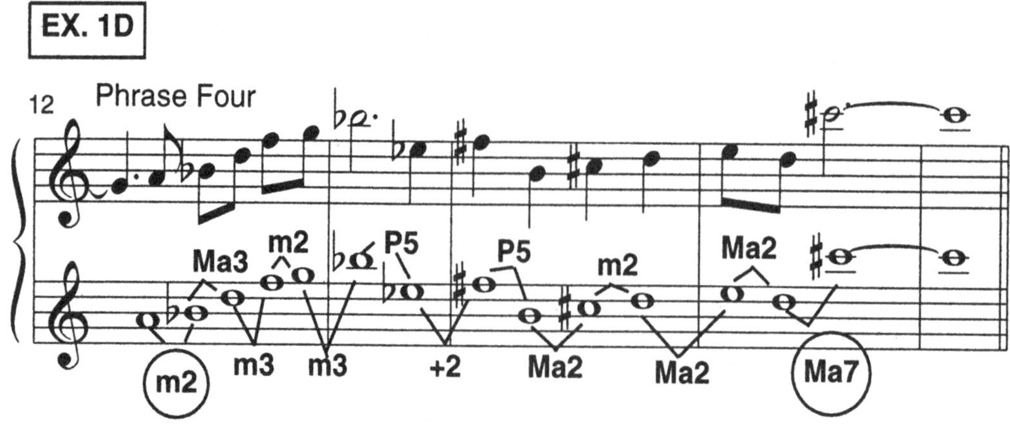

Beginning Section B, Bill composes two two-measure phrases back to back, both containing the same intervallic breakdown and both continuing the tension from phrase four by ending on a Ma7th. Here, Bill is shortening the phrase lengths by shortening theme patterns, liquidating the theme, and rightly so. This is the second half of the theme (or Section B). Notice also that the interval pattern in measure 17 rhythmically speeds up (DIMINUTION) in measure 19.

Section B

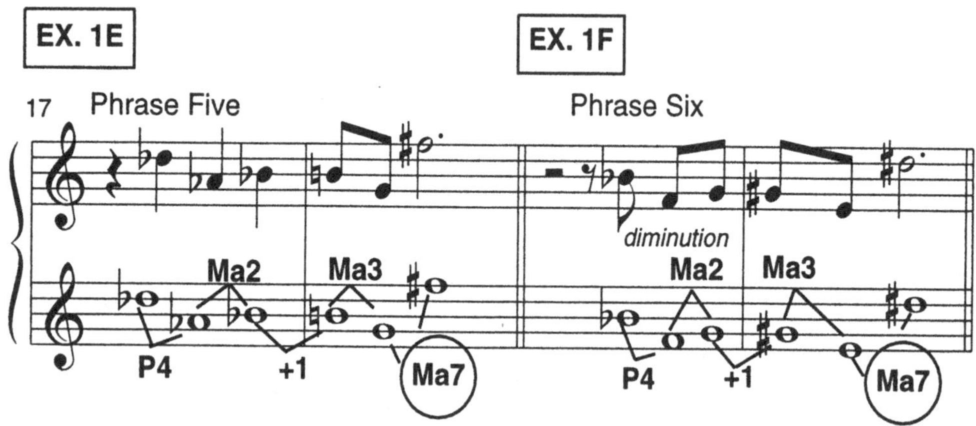

Diminution occurs again in this three-measure phrase. Measure 21 rhythmically speeds up in measure 22, last half. At measure 23, things get very calm with a minor 3rd ("f" to "d") and a perfect 5th ("d" to "a"). Measure 23 also spells out the D minor triad; in fact, a keen observer would notice two more minor triads in this phrase: measure 21, C# minor triad and measure 22, A minor triad.

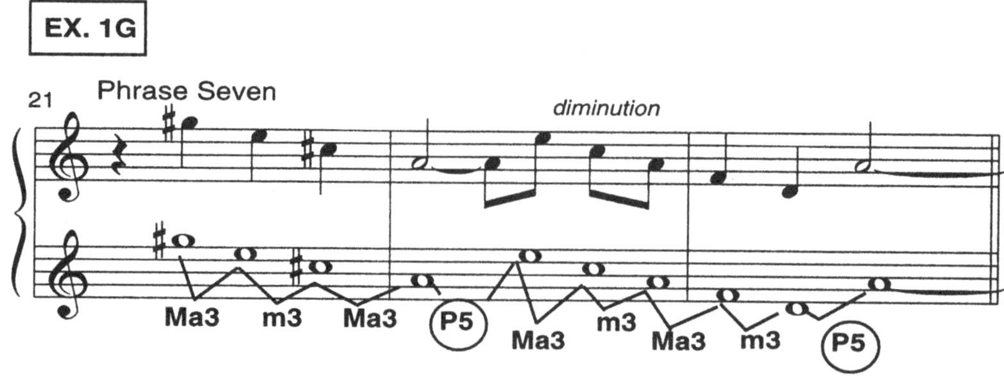

Phrase eight is full of goodies. We have another example of EXTENSION, but this time Bill gives us SPACE in the middle by sitting on the whole note "a" in measure 25. Repeat the experiment we did at the end of Section A and you'll see (hear) that we don't really miss measure 25. At measure 24, we have the intervallic inversion of measure 17. And, for the first time, in measure 26 we have an example of the retrograde inversion of measure 23! Phrase eight is further liquidating the theme, with final note serving both as the leading tone of the B minor mode (spelled enharmonically here; the original score has a B-flat) and the perfect "turn back" effect to measure 1 on the "f#," or to an improvisation.

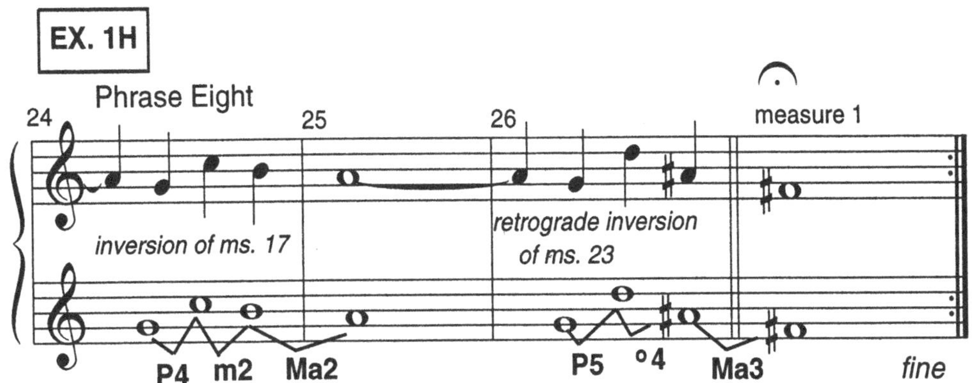

"FUNNY MAN" & "I SHOULD CARE"

The subject of reharmonization begins with a brief discussion of tonality and what is available to us in the major/minor system. I refer to this as our vocabulary: scales and chords.

There are fifteen major scales and their corresponding relative minors, making a grand total of thirty. Tonality is a synthesis of modality; therefore, all the old modes (Ionian, Dorian, etc.) are included in this system plus some wonderful new things, like the harmonic system.

With the harmonic system we can construct a chord from each degree of each of our thirty major and minor scales. These are triads, sevenths, ninths, elevenths, and thirteenths. The grand total of chords available to us is 3, 390!

A theory of harmony involves a lot more than memorizing the above vocabulary. It involves key relationships, chord functions and progressions, phrase construction, modulation, melodic invention, voice leading using four to six-part chords, altered chords, counterpoint, and finally composition. Now it's at this final stage—composition—that reharmonization begins. You must develop a sensitive ear, become knowledgeable and experienced with all the above before I would trust you with a reharmonization of any tune, even a blues!! One change of harmony affects the entire piece. That's the reason why, with Bill's tunes, one does not reharmonize them; they are complete compositions. A reharmonization means you've chosen a better chord than the composer wrote. Quite a responsibility, I'd say!

Arnold Schoenberg, in his 1911 *Theory of Harmony* text, uses the phrase, "Borrowed from the key of..." As I discuss the reharmonization by Bill Evans of "I Should Care," and compare it to "Funny Man," I will apply this Schoenbergian concept of key relationships. Keys are either closely or distantly related by fifths. "I Should Care" is in the key of C Major, the tonic key. One fifth higher (adding one sharp) is the key of G Major, the dominant key of C Major. Travelling one fifth lower (adding one flat) we arrive at F major, the subdominant key of C Major. By including in your thinking their relative minors, we have A minor, E minor, and D minor respectively. These six keys (and scales) are all closely related, and in "I Should Care" C Major is the tonic key, A minor its relative minor, G Major its dominant key, E minor its relative minor, F Major the subdominant key, and D minor its relative minor. Schoenberg calls these six keys the *diatonic regions* (see EX. 1).

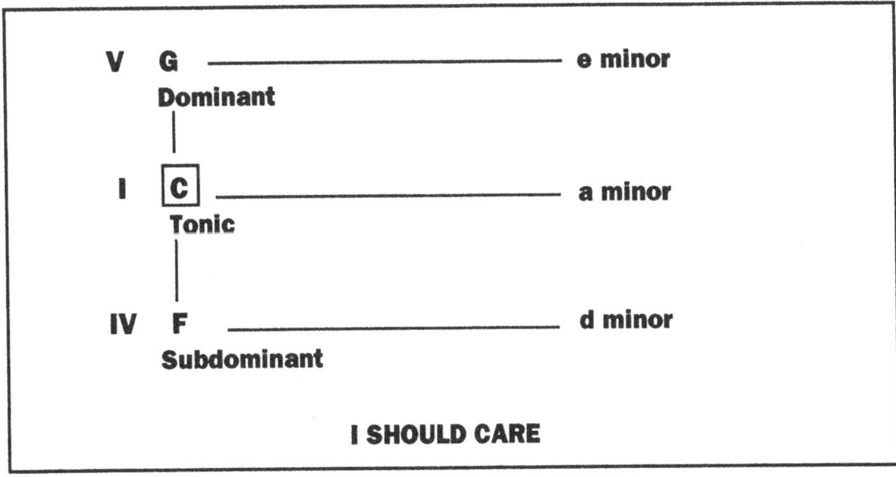

Therefore, we can tastefully choose any chord constructed on the scale degrees from these six regions (keys) for a reharmonization to "I Should Care." Using the Theory of Harmony chart (see EX. 2) gives us a vocabulary of twenty-one chords from the C, G, and F regions, and forty-eight chords from their relative minor regions.

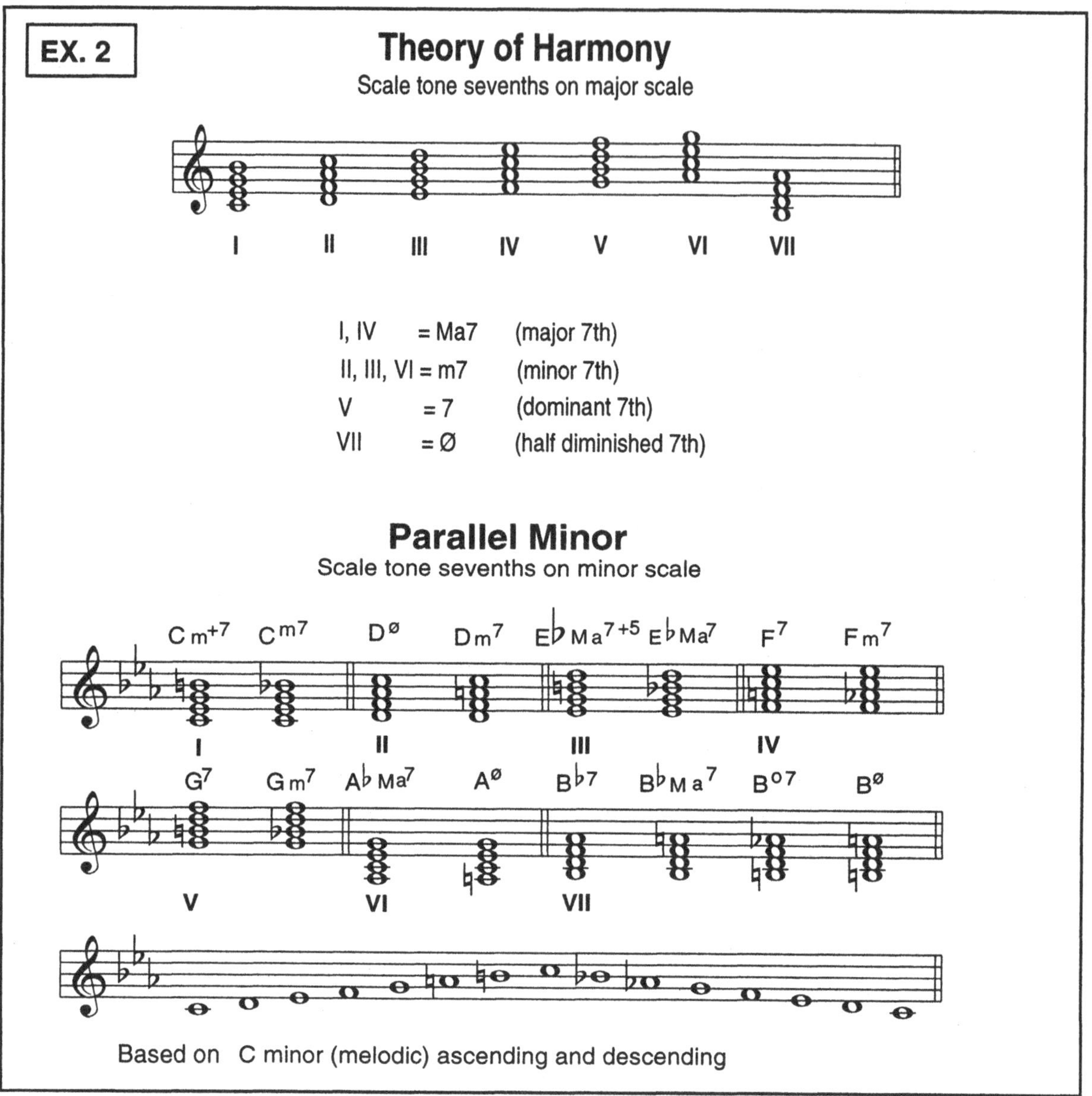

In the first four measures, I compare the original chords with the reharmonizations as they relate to the diatonic regions (see EX. 3).

EX. 3

Original Chords	Dm7 G7	Cma7 Am7	Dm7 G7	Cma7
Bill's Reharmonization (alt. = altered)	F#7 B7 alt.	Emi9 alt. A7 alt.	Dm9 alt. G7 alt.	Cma7 +11 F7 alt.

In measure one, the F#7 is the tritone substitute for C7; the C7 is borrowed from the region of F Major. B7 is borrowed from the E minor region. In measure two, the Em9 is borrowed from the tonic region, C Major (the ninth is sharped and comes from the G Major scale); A7 is borrowed from the D minor region. There is no reharmonization in all of measure three and the first half of measure four. Bill adds an F7 in the second half of measure four to keep the momentum going; F7 is the tritone substitute of B7, which is borrowed from the region of E minor. By following the concept "borrowed from the key of . . .", and the concept of tritone substitution, you will be able to relate all the reharmonizations to the diatonic regions of C Major for "I Should Care."

Why chords function the way they do is the very foundation of all theory, and the understanding of such is crucial to any successful reharmonization of standard tunes. One reharmonization can change the entire mood of the piece by either destroying or enhancing it. One does not substitute a chord for the original, one reharmonizes. There are no substitute chords: they are either right or wrong according to the theory derived from the Masters. The tritone substitute is not a reharmonization because it resolves to the same chord. For example, C7 can resolve down a half step (chromatic function), and its tritone substitute, F#7, resolves down a fifth (tonic to dominant function) to the same chord.

With "Funny Man," we're not talking about reharmonization, but composition. Bill's songs are more complex than the standard songs, and for me they bridge the gap between the small song form (aba) to the larger forms (sonata, scherzo, etc.). For a study of form, I refer you to Schoenberg's *Fundamentals of Music Composition.*

Schoenberg introduces the concept, tonic minor (parallel minor), subdominant minor and dominant minor relationships to the original key as a means for acquiring more chromatically related chords, for inventing progressions or, in our case, for the reharmonization of standards. The secret is to be able to hear the tension of all these key relationships against the tonic key and to understand the function of all the diatonic chords and the chromatic chords that are available. Then reharmonization becomes very creative, exciting and above all, easy!

Having said all the above, I shall leave you to analyze on your own the chords of "Funny Man" and how they relate to the diatonic and chromatic regions (see EX. 4). Any chord the root of which is out of the scale of the tonic key and the diatonic regions is to be considered derived from the chromatic regions.

EX. 4

Parallel minor with relative major		Diatonic Region		Parallel Major with relative minor	
Db	Bbm	Bb	Gm	G	Em
Gb	Ebm	**[Eb]**	Cm	C	Am
Cb	Abm	Ab	Fm	F	Dm

All the chords of "Funny Man" can be related to the above diatonic and chromatic regions

"Funny Man"

4 Part Realization by Jack Reilly

Music by Bill Evans

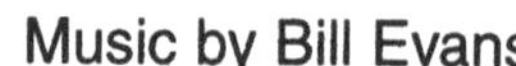

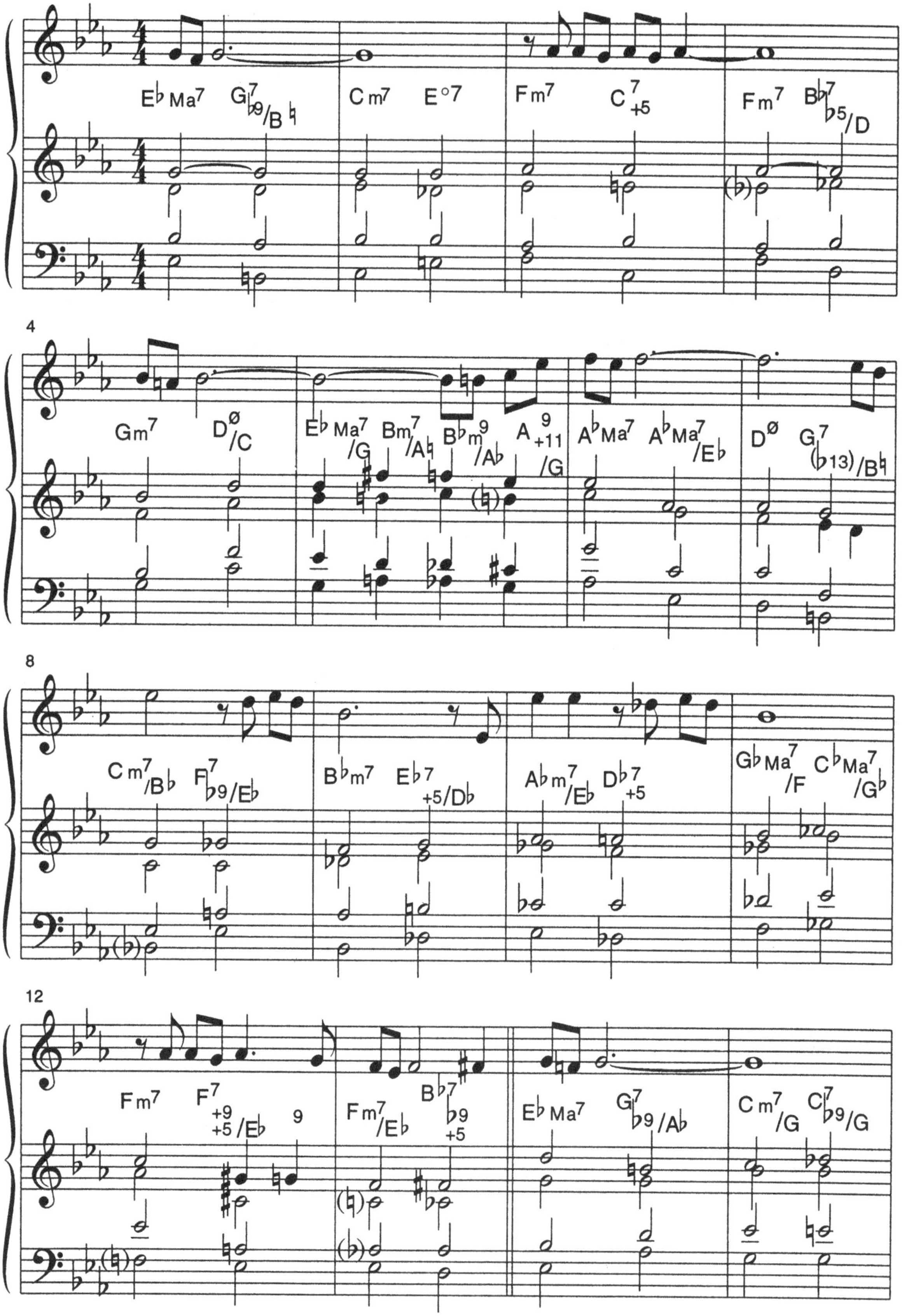

16
Fm7/A♭
C7 ♭9 ♭13 /B♭
Fm7/C
F♯o7/C
Gm7/B♭
Cm7/B♭
19
B7 +5/F×
Em7
Aø
D9/F♯
G Ma9/B♮
C Ma7
Fm7/E♭
C7 +5/E♮
23
(Turn Around:)
Fm7
B♭9 +5/D
E♭ Ma7
C7 ♭9/E♮
Fm7
B♭7 ♭9 +5/A♭
E♭ Ma7/D

I Should Care
Sammy Cahn
A. Stordahl
Paul Weston
1
F♯7♭9 B 9 13 Em9 A7 ♭9 +11 13 Dm11 G 9 +11 13 CMa 9 +11 F 9 +11 13
5
Eø9 B♭ 9 +11 13 Asus A7 ♭9 ♭5 ♭13 Dm9 Em9 Fm9 B♭ 9 13
9
CMa7 C 9 13 ♭5 Bø7 11 E 7 +9 ♭13 Gm9 C7 +9 ♭9 +11 FMa9
13
Bø11 E7 ♭5 ♭9 ♭13 Am 9 11 E7 ♭9 +5 Am 9 11 D 13 ♭5 Dm9 G 13 ♭5

F♯7 ♭9 ♭5
B7 ♭9 ♭13
E m9
A7 ♭9 +5
D m9
G9 sus4 +5 -3
C Ma 7 9 6
F 13 ♭5
17
E ø
B♭ 9 +11
A sus
A7 ♭9 ♭5
D m9
E m9
F m9
B♭7 ♭9 +9 +11 13
21
C Ma 7 9 6
C 9 +11
B ø 13
E7 +9 ♭5 ♭13
A m9 +7
D 9 +11 13
25
D m9
A7 +9 +5 +11
D 9 13 ♭5
G sus
G7 ♭9 13 +11
C Ma9
F Ma9
E m7
A m7
29
3 3 3 3 3 3
fine

I FALL IN LOVE TOO EASILY

Let us remember that a reharmonization must replace the original chord with something better. The term "better" could be defined as more interesting, more dissonant, more consonant, or that it gives us the "feeling" of roving into another region (key). In other words, there must be a sound reason for choosing the reharmonization and it must not destroy the melodic tension or drama, but, rather, it must enhance melodic tension or drama. This is a very demanding task, and one must be aware of all the possibilities, both obvious and not so.

For this article, I take you step by step, measure by measure, through the entire progression in order to shed some light on Bill's thought processes with regard to the choice of a "better" chord, and to gain more insight into this fascinating and much-maligned or abused subject, reharmonization.

The first step is to determine what other keys are suggested or can be suggested by the original progression. Most of the standard tunes that are part of the jazz musician's repertoire were written before 1950 and are, therefore, very diatonic, i.e. they modulate or suggest keys (regions) that are closely related to the original key.

This tune is in the key of G Major. That means the closely related keys are D Major and C Major, and their three relative minors: E minor, B minor, and A minor. The secondary dominants are A7, G7, B7, F#7, and E7. The term "secondary dominant" is another way of saying "the fifth of." So A7 is the fifth of D Major; G7 is the fifth of C Major; B7 is the fifth of E minor; F#7 is the fifth of B minor; and E7 is the fifth of A minor. These secondary dominants destroy or weaken the original key!! When we alter these chords, i.e. flat the fifth, add a ninth, raise the fifth, etc., we give them more power and energy (dissonance) and further weaken the key center or tonic, but strengthen the new one. Schoenberg teaches us that the VII, III+ and IIø chords can also <u>function</u> like a secondary dominant, that is, weaken the original key center and/or enrich the diatonic progression. The VII chord is diminished, the III+ is augmented and the IIø is half-diminished; these are dissonant (active) chords. The IIø and III+ belong to the minor scale. The VII chord is half-diminished in both major and minor, but is a full diminished only in the minor scale.

To summarize: in the key of G Major, we have available all the diatonic chords belonging to the scales of G Major, E minor, D Major, B minor, C Major, and A minor.

Now I can begin to justify every chord Bill used in this reharmonization as being "borrowed from" one of the diatonic regions of the original.

The original key is G Major. The chords in measures 3 and 5 belong to the region of E minor and prepare the arrival of the modulation to the relative minor of G Major at measure 9. The E minor key then functions as the dominant minor of A minor which arises in measure 12. The final phrase (beginning at measure 13) jumps to the relative major (C) of A minor to begin the descent to G Major via two secondary dominants, B7 and E7 in measure 14.

The turn-around (measure 16) is the most interesting measure for me: every quarter note pulse has a substitute chord. On the downbeat, instead of the I (tonic chord), we get the VIIø7 of D major; beat two is a C m7, the only non-diatonic chord in the entire progression. It's borrowed from the key of G minor, parallel minor, three fifths removed from the original key. On the third beat, Bill uses the perfect substitute for a tonic chord, the III7, Bm7. And on the fourth beat, Bill places his favorite tension chord, a secondary dominant seventh, flat nine, plus nine, augmented eleventh chord built on the second degree of the G Major scale. Most fake books would label it a Bbo7 chord. That is misleading and does not give us any real insight into why this chord functions the way it does. It's an altered II chord, functioning as a secondary dominant on its return to the dominant region of the key in measure 1.

In the second ending, Bill creates the feeling of a tag or extension by the use of secondary dominants, again borrowed from the diatonic regions of A minor and B minor. And as a complete surprise, he ends the tune with a super-powerful progression—II7, I7 (Am7 to GMa7)—with a brilliant idea: to make a cadenza on the Am7. When I play this tune, I end on EMa7 in the final measure instead of GMa7. The Am7 then functions as a IV minor chord of E Major, creating the "feel" of a plagal cadence: IV (A minor) to I (E Major).

I Fall In Love Too Easily

Voicings by Jack Reilly

Music by Jule Styne
Lyric by Sammy Cahn

TWELVE TONE TUNE

The number 12 is associated with the cosmic law of the cycle, or the patterns of the cycle, which is the zodiac. In certain esoteric traditions, the number 12 also refers to the sign Libra and is associated with justice, balance, and harmony, but it can also, in a different context, refer to the sign Pisces, the 12th sign of the zodiac.

In tonal music, we have 12 keys, each one containing 12 half steps within the octave. The chromatic scale consists of 12 half steps. A universal form in jazz is the blues, 12 bars in length, divided in 3 phrases, 4 measures for each phrase.

Atonality gives equal weight (tonal gravity) to each of the 12 tones of the chromatic scale. There is no key center, and, therefore, no key signature. Atonal compositions are based on the 12-note "series" or "twelve tone row." It is not unusual for atonal compositions to be based on more than one row. Schoenberg's music evolved from Bach, through Wagner and on to atonality.

In "T.T.T." (Twelve Tone Tune), Bill composed one twelve tone row, repeated it three times (94 measure phrases for each repetition), changed the register and rhythmic grouping in each phrase and then added harmony. See EX. 1 for the composition of the row and EX. 2 for the melodic grouping in 3 phrases (4 + 4 + 4).

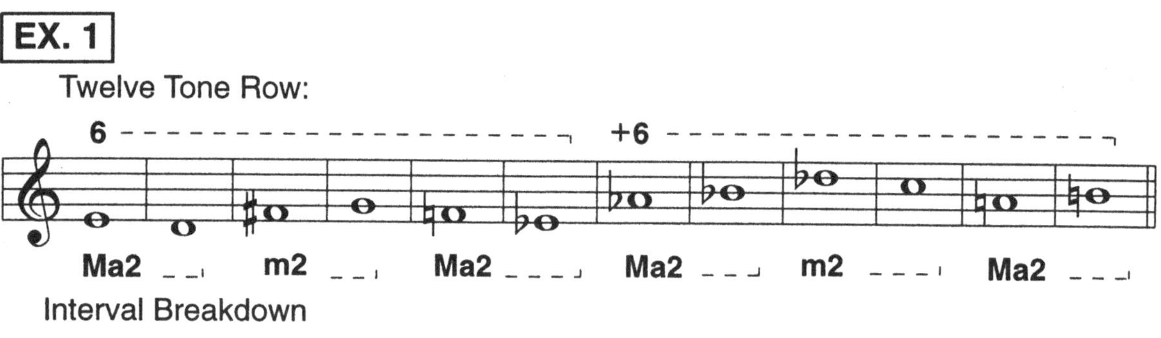

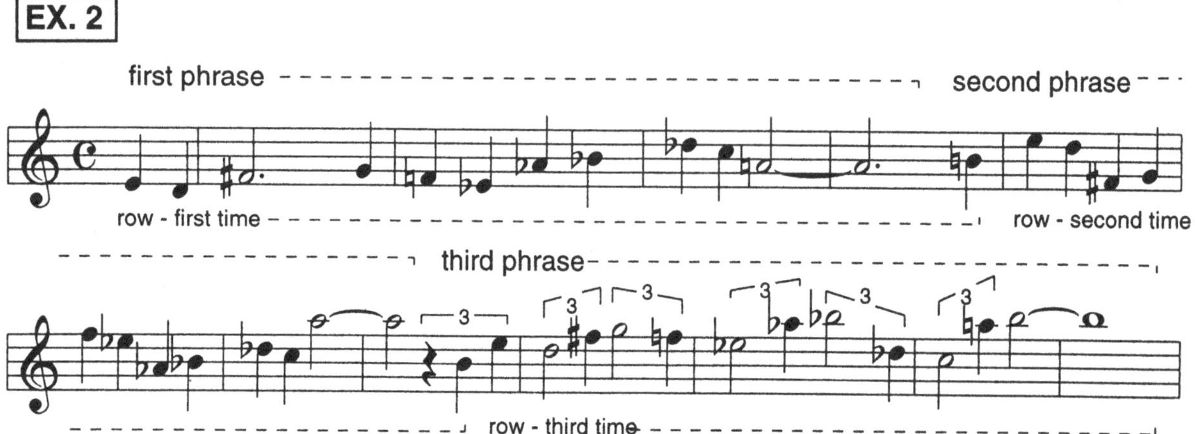

EX. 3 is a 4-part voicing based on Bill's harmonization of the row.

EX. 4 is a transcription of the first statement of the tune from the duo album with Eddie Gomez entitled "Intuition." EX. 5 is my chart.

EX. 4 **Twelve Tone Tune**

Twelve Tone Tune

Voicings by Jack Reilly

By Bill Evans

HOW DEEP IS THE OCEAN

This is an AA tune. It divides itself into 16 + 16, adding up to 32 measures. Another way to look at the form is to think in 8-bar phrases: 8 + 8 + 8. Expressing this division in letter symbols, I come up with ABAC. This is a more precise analysis and serves as a mnemonic device to assist the improviser in memorizing the progression. This is not a tune for a beginner in improvisation, especially when one compares the original harmony with Evans' reharmonization.

The song begins in the key of C minor and ends in the relative major, E-flat. If you have a copy of the original sheet music, you'll discover that Irving Berlin uses only one chord per measure for most of the 32 bars. His genius lies in the bass line he has created. Through the use of inversions, he passes from C minor (3 flats), measures 1–4, to the region of G minor (2 flats) in measures 5–8. In measures 9-16 (Letter B), Berlin uses four secondary dominants. This is another stroke of genius, for he creates just enough tension to avoid another tonal center — a brilliant contrast to the restful tonic feeling of Letter A. Letter B works its way back to the V7 chord of C minor (G7), preparing us for the exact repetition of Letter A. In Letter C, measures 25–32, Berlin settles down, but this time passing through F minor (4 flats), measures 25–28, and concluding in E-flat Major (3 flats), measures 29–32.

Take a look at the chordal breakdown from the Berlin original piano chart in EX. 1.

EX. 1

Cm	Cm B bass	Cm Bb bass	Am7 b5 D7
Gm	Gm F# bass	Gm7	Bb7 Ab bass
Eb7	Eb7	Ab7	Ab7
Cm7b5	F7+5	Bb7+5	G7+5

Coda

Gm b5	C7 b5	Fm	Abm6
Eb Bb bass	F9 A bass	Bb7	Eb

Let's compare immediately Evans' chordal chart in EX. 2. This analysis coincides with my voicing realization in EX. 3.

EX. 2 [Read left to right, line by line.]

Cm9+7 Cm11	Aø11 Bbm11	Dø11 b13 Aø b9 b13	G7 b9 b13 D7 b5 b9 b13
Gm+7,9,13 Gm11	Eø11, b13 C7+5+11	Aø b9 b13 Fm11	D7 b5+5 b9 Bb7+5+9+11
Eb9, +11,13 Ab13	B9, +11,13 Em11	Bbm13 Ebm11	Eb7, b9,+9,13 Ab13
C#m11 Bb+5+9+11	F#13 A7, b9, b13	Cø11 D7 b9+9, 13	F7,+5,+9,+11 G7+9 b13

Coda

Eb9sus Fm9, 11	Db9sus Fm13	C7,b9sus, b13 Abm11	C7 b5 b9 Db13
EbMa9 B9, +5 +4	G7 +9, b9 Bb9+5,+11	Cm9,11 Eb6/9	F13 G7 b5 b9 b13

My comparison of Berlin's original harmony with Evans' reharmonization is to remind me that a composer's original scorc, usually the published sheet music, will always reveal the genius, if it's there. Great tunes were great tunes before any jazz player reharmonized them!!! A composer worth his salt will never, never reharmonize his own tunes. A great song is conceived in its entirety; that is to say, the melody, harmony, pulse or meter, bass line, and rhythmic motifs are heard in the creative musical ear and mind *simultaneously*. If you can't hear it all at once, you're not a composer, and should step down. Reharmonization is not meant to change the character and personality of a great tune. Substituting different chords is not what I call reharmonizing. When I reharmonize, I enter into the mood (also the mode) of the song. This usually takes years of playing the tune in the original form and key. Reharmonization should enhance the melody—make it stand out more. Reharmonization should make a celebration of modulation; the arrival of a new key center or region can be explored a thousand different ways, and, if done with taste, it never—*never*!!—destroys the composer's original intent. Therein lies the secret: *intentionality*. To be able to discern the composer's intention takes great humility, but also complete knowledge of the past. And I don't mean only knowledge of the American Popular Song; I mean also knowledge of Western Classical Music. There isn't a progression in the jazz literature or the pop repertoire that hasn't already been written in classical music. The Liszt "B Minor Sonata" covers seventy per cent of all progressions found in mainstream jazz tunes.

How Deep Is The Ocean

(How High Is The Sky)

Reharmonized by Bill Evans

Voicings by Jack Reilly

Words and Music by
Irving Berlin

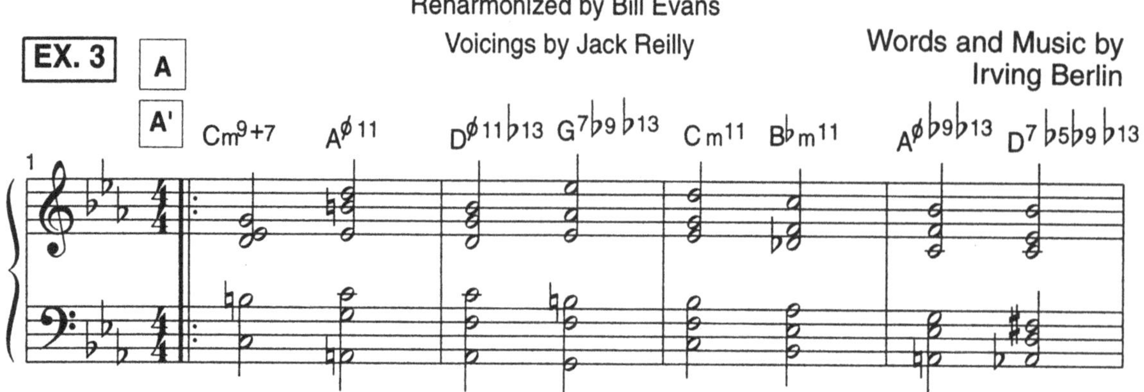

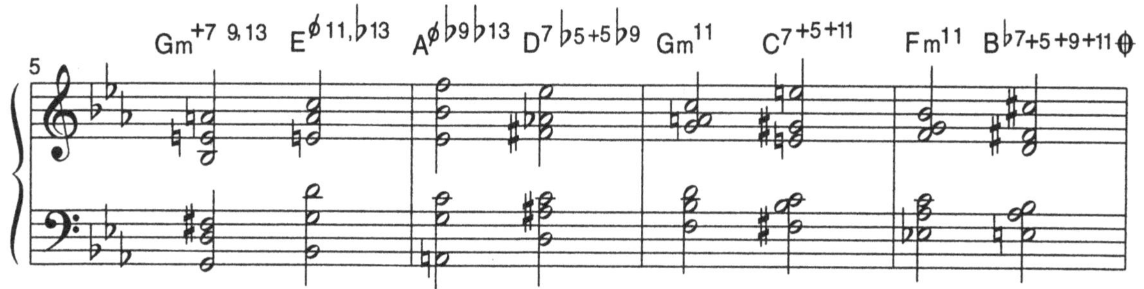

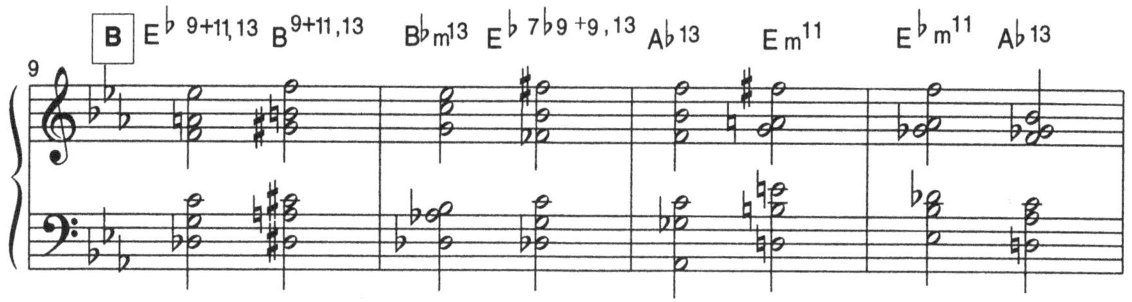

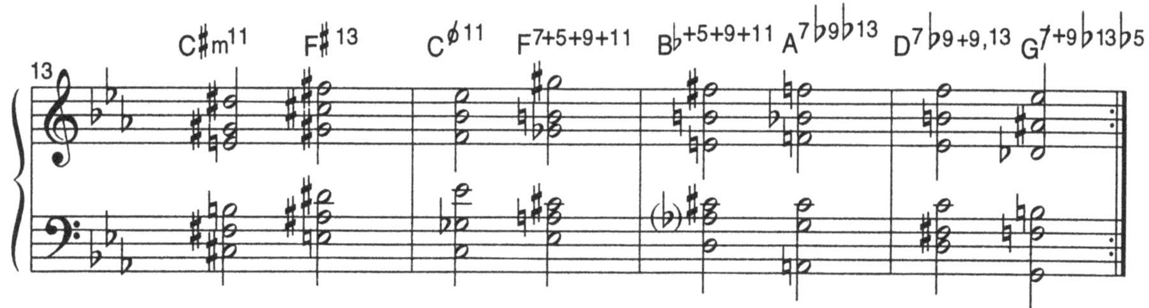

Bill's reharmonization of "How Deep Is The Ocean" is a tour de force. He enriches Letter A by surrounding the tonalities of C minor (measures 1–4) and G minor (measures 5–8) with diatonic chords. In Letter B, he creates more tension with chromatic secondary sevenths. And in Letter C, he highlights the arrival of F minor and the final resting place, E-flat Major, with both chromatic embellishing chords and diatonic approaches to Berlin's original score. A 6-part voicing arrangement of Bill's masterpiece was the only format I could use to fully justify his reharmonization. When I practice this chorale realization of "How Deep," I always have the feeling, "How obvious. . .why didn't I think of that chord in measure 25?"

We have a lot to be grateful for: Bill Evans left us many beautiful compositions, but also many beautiful renditions of the great standards. And don't forget, they were great standards before he touched them.

B MINOR WALTZ

If you have been studying and following these voicing articles, you have observed that the challenge is not in choosing a good vertical arrangement of parts (voices), but in their linear motion; that is, the way each voice connects melodically. The mood of the piece is captured and enhanced by this process. For me, these voicing layouts, or chorales as I call them, open the doors of perception. They ease the way for the improviser to play on the structures when encountering Evans' tunes. I would say this discipline is mandatory.

Regarding "B Minor Waltz," the rewards for this writer were greater than the sum of its parts. I fully appreciated the uniqueness of the piece upon completing this voicing chart, memorizing it and then practicing it. It was the drama and tension between the A and B sections that were giving me problems, however. Let's take a look.

Part A is 18 measures long and Part B, 15. This tells us absolutely nothing. We must analyze the phrase structure (sentences) of A and B and then compare. Here's the breakdown.

PART A:	Phrase One	Measures 1 - 4
	Phrase Two	Measures 5 - 8
	Phrase Three	Measures 9 - 12
	Phrase Four	Measures 13 - 14
	Phrase Five	Measure 15
	Phrase Six	Measures 16 - 18

PART B:	Phrase One	Measures 19 - 22
	Phrase Two	Measures 23 - 25
	Phrase Three	Measures 26 - 29
	Phrase Four	Measures 30 - 33

Can you see why I was having problems? The memory must come first before this tune can be considered ready for practicing. Now we can reduce the phrase lengths to single digits in order to *hear* the progressions in sentences. This gives us:

PART A: 4 + 4 + 4 + 2 + 1 + 3

PART B: 4 + 3 + 4 + 4

You can now practice each phrase or sentence separately, gradually piecing them together until you can sustain an improvisation for the full 33 bars. The practice time can be made even more concentrated by focusing your attention on the linear motion of each part in EX. 1.

B Minor Waltz

(For Elaine)

6-Part Voicings by Jack Reilly

Ex. 1, B Minor Waltz, contd.

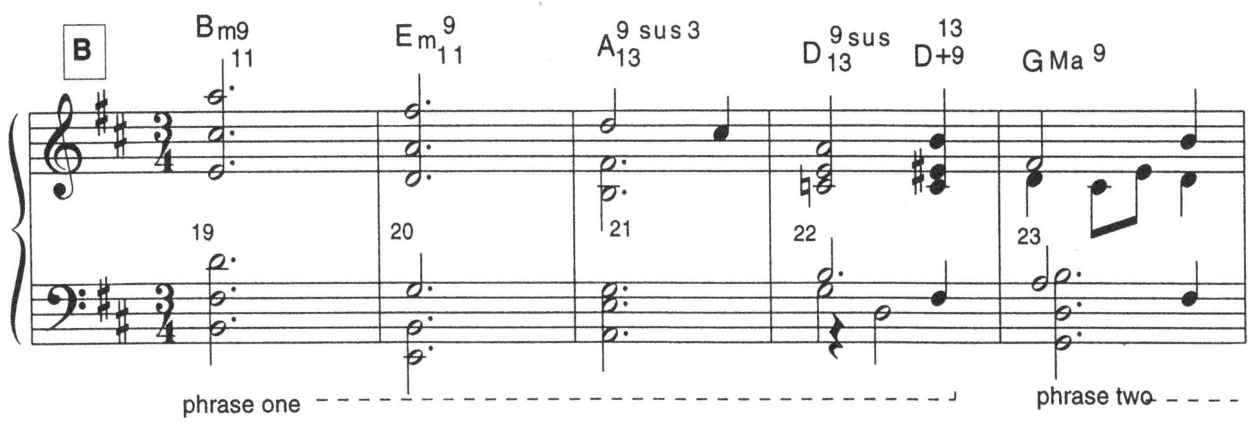

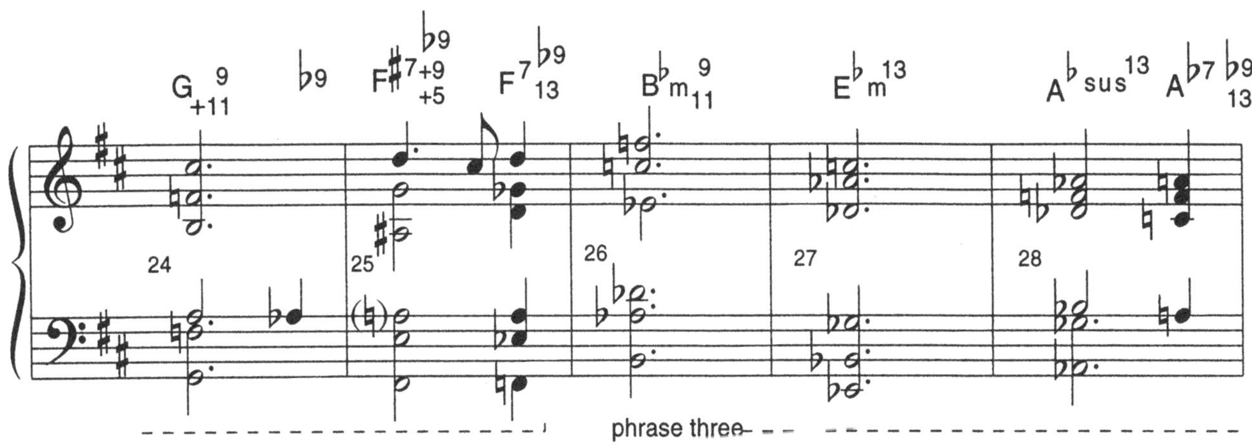

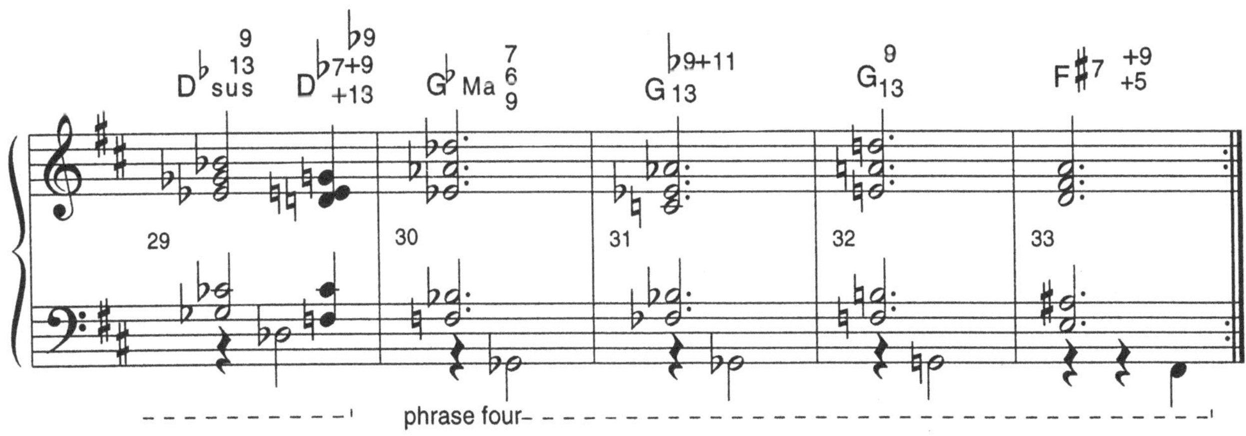

By treating the 6-part voicing as six separate and different melodies-in-embryonic-form, you can try ornamentation techniques to create an improvisation. To illustrate, I have improvised two melodies around the soprano part (EX. 2).

EX. 2 **B Minor Waltz**

Continue this type of exercise for the other parts: 2nd soprano, alto, tenor, 2nd tenor, and bass. You will notice that my 6-part voicing chart takes on the characteristics of a Bach chorale because of the contrapuntal interplay between the voices. See particularly measures 15, 16, 17, and 18, where the alto voice in measures 15 and 16 is freely imitated in the tenor part in 16–17. Then the soprano part in 17–18 continues the imitation (See EX. 3 for a clear picture of this contrapuntal device).

EX. 3

The imitation in the tenor begins where the alto ends; but the soprano imitation is in *stretto;* that is, it overlaps or begins before the tenor finishes its imitation. In fugue composition, stretto usually comes near the end of the fugue. Notice the interest it generates here at the end of Part A of EX. 1.

In EX. 4, I have given you a basic (elementary) example of transforming the harmony (the vertical layout) into scales (the horizontal layout). This is common practice among horn players and greatly facilitates improvising (creating melodies) on the chord changes. After all, a scale or mode is a melody in embryonic form.

The art of chorale composition, writing voicing charts, using contrapuntal devices, modes, and scales, I lump under the broad category, *vocabulary.* All this knowledge and technique does not guarantee a musical result, but it sure helps develop and cultivate the ear.

EX. 4 **Scale Studies for B Minor Waltz**

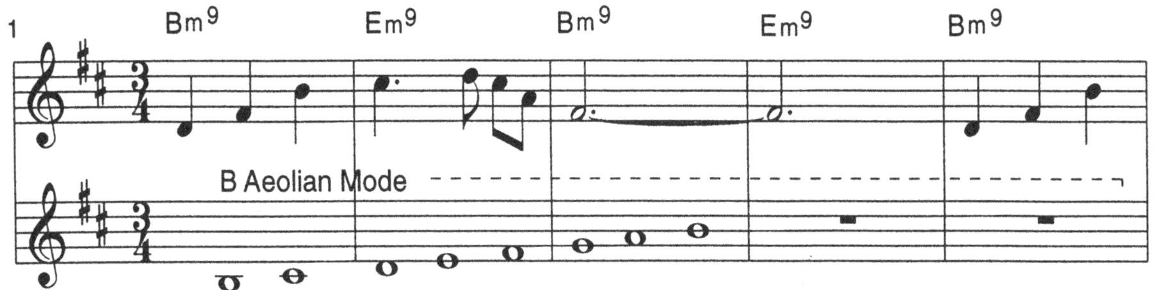

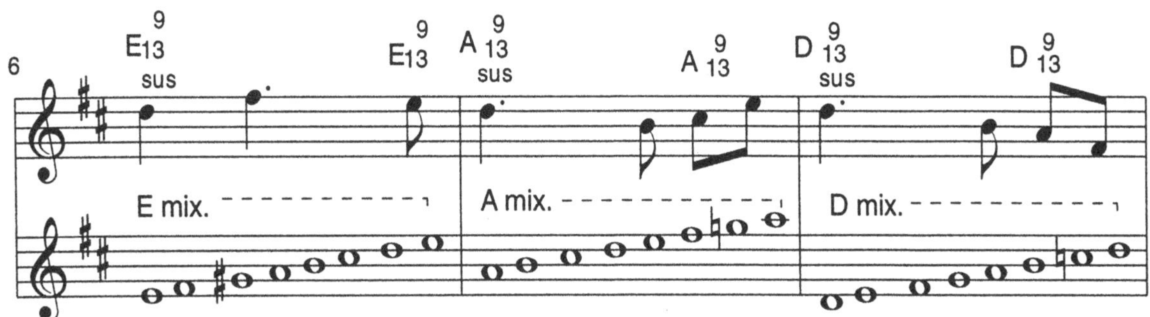

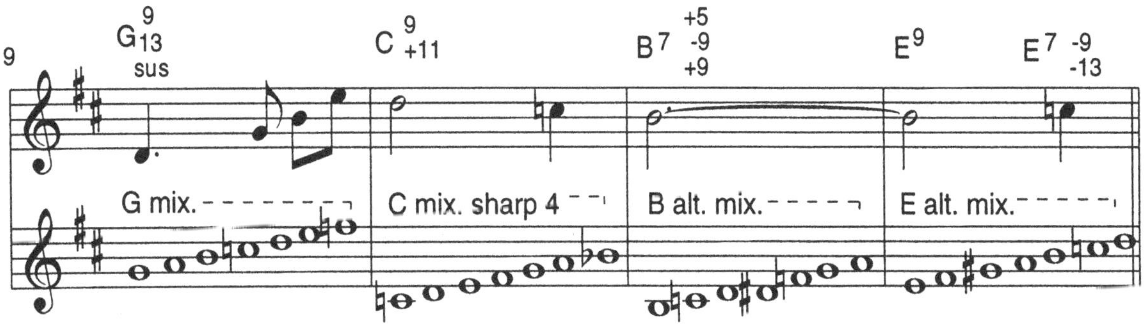

[mix.=Mixolydian Mode]

ABOUT THE AUTHOR

Since 1949, Jack Reilly's career as pianist, composer, author, and educator has co-existed within the apparently opposing poles of jazz and classical music. Born in 1932 on Staten Island, New York, Reilly began classical piano studies at the age of seven. In his teens he led a big band, getting his first taste of jazz playing the music of Duke Ellington, Benny Goodman, Count Basie, and Woody Herman. After serving in the Navy, he majored in composition, theory, and piano at Manhattan School of Music, graduating with a Masters Degree in 1958.

His compositions include *Jazz Requiem* (1968), *Oratorio* (1974), *Chuang-Tzu - Theme and Eight Variations for Orchestra* (1993), *Concertina for Jazz Piano and Strings, Lullabys for Orchestra, Fantasy for Piano and Wind Quintet, Piano Sonata in D Minor,* and *Concerto for Harmonica and Strings*. In 2001, his *Piano Concerto-Orbitals* was premiered with the composer as soloist with the Keweenaw Symphony.

Mr. Reilly has seven CDs and four videos on the Unichrom label, and has toured and recorded with Ben Webster, Joe Maneri, George Russell, John LaPorta, and Sheila Jordan, among many other artists. He has chaired the Jazz Studies Departments of the New England Conservatory of Music, Mannes College of Music, and The New School; he is presently Jazz Piano Professor at Rowan College, Glassboro, New Jersey.

In addition to this publication, his other music folios are: *Jazz Piano Solos* (arrangements of standards, also published by Hal Leonard Corporation 00310159), and *Species Blues*, a three volume treatise on jazz piano improvisation.

ARTIST TRANSCRIPTIONS®

Artist Transcriptions are authentic, note-for-note transcriptions of today's hottest artists in jazz, pop and rock. These outstanding, accurate arrangements are in an easy-to-read format which includes all essential lines. **Artist Transcriptions** can be used to perform, sequence or for reference.

FLUTE

00672379 Eric Dolphy Collection $19.95
00672582 The Very Best of James Galway . $19.99
00672372 James Moody Collection – Sax and Flute $19.95

GUITAR & BASS

00660113 Guitar Style of George Benson $19.99
00672573 Ray Brown – Legendary Jazz Bassist $22.99
00672331 Ron Carter Collection $24.99
00660115 Al Di Meola – Friday Night in San Francisco $24.99
00125617 Best of Herb Ellis $19.99
00699306 Jim Hall – Exploring Jazz Guitar .. $19.99
00672353 The Joe Pass Collection $22.99
00673216 John Patitucci $22.99
00672374 Johnny Smith – Guitar Solos $24.99

PIANO & KEYBOARD

00672487 Monty Alexander Plays Standards $19.95
00672520 Count Basie Collection $19.95
00192307 Bebop Piano Legends $19.99
00113680 Blues Piano Legends $22.99
00672526 The Bill Charlap Collection $19.99
00278003 A Charlie Brown Christmas $19.99
00672300 Chick Corea – Paint the World $19.99
00146105 Bill Evans – Alone $21.99
00672548 The Mastery of Bill Evans $16.99
00672365 Bill Evans – Play Standards $22.99
00121885 Bill Evans – Time Remembered . $22.99
00672510 Bill Evans Trio Vol. 1: 1959-1961 $29.99
00672511 Bill Evans Trio Vol. 2: 1962-1965 .. $27.99
00672512 Bill Evans Trio Vol. 3: 1968-1974 . $29.99
00672513 Bill Evans Trio Vol. 4: 1979-1980 . $24.95
00193332 Erroll Garner – Concert by the Sea $22.99
00672486 Vince Guaraldi Collection $19.99
00289644 The Definitive Vince Guaraldi $39.99
00672419 Herbie Hancock Collection $24.99
00672438 Hampton Hawes Collection $19.95
00672322 Ahmad Jamal Collection $27.99
00255671 Jazz Piano Masterpieces $22.99
00124367 Jazz Piano Masters Play Rodgers & Hammerstein $19.99
00672564 Best of Jeff Lorber $19.99
00672476 Brad Mehldau Collection $24.99
00672388 Best of Thelonious Monk $24.99
00672389 Thelonious Monk Collection $24.99
00672390 Thelonious Monk Plays Jazz Standards – Volume 1 .... $24.99
00672391 Thelonious Monk Plays Jazz Standards – Volume 2 .... $24.99
00264094 Oscar Peterson – Night Train $22.99
00672544 Oscar Peterson – Originals $17.99
00672531 Oscar Peterson – Plays Duke Ellington $27.99
00672563 Oscar Peterson – A Royal Wedding Suite $19.99
00672569 Oscar Peterson – Tracks $19.99
00672533 Oscar Peterson – Trios $39.99
00672534 Very Best of Oscar Peterson $29.99
00672371 Bud Powell Classics $22.99
00672376 Bud Powell Collection $24.99
00672507 Gonzalo Rubalcaba Collection ... $19.95
00672316 Art Tatum Collection $27.99
00672355 Art Tatum Solo Book $22.99
00672357 The Billy Taylor Collection $24.95
00673215 McCoy Tyner $22.99
00672321 Cedar Walton Collection $19.95
00672519 Kenny Werner Collection $19.95

SAXOPHONE

00672566 The Mindi Abair Collection $14.99
00673244 Julian "Cannonball" Adderley Collection $22.99
00673237 Michael Brecker $24.99
00672429 Michael Brecker Collection $24.99
00672529 John Coltrane – Giant Steps $22.99
00672494 John Coltrane – A Love Supreme $17.99
00672493 John Coltrane Plays "Coltrane Changes" $19.95
00672453 John Coltrane Plays Standards .. $25.99
00673233 John Coltrane Solos $29.99
00672328 Paul Desmond Collection $22.99
00672530 Kenny Garrett Collection $24.99
00699375 Stan Getz $24.99
00672377 Stan Getz – Bossa Novas $24.99
00673254 Great Tenor Sax Solos $22.99
00672523 Coleman Hawkins Collection $24.99
00673239 Best of Kenny G $22.99
00673229 Kenny G – Breathless $19.99
00672462 Kenny G – Classics in the Key of G $26.99
00672485 Kenny G – Faith: A Holiday Album . $17.99
00672373 Kenny G – The Moment $22.99
00672498 Jackie McLean Collection $19.95
00672372 James Moody Collection – Sax and Flute $19.95
00672539 Gerry Mulligan Collection $24.99
00102751 Sonny Rollins, Art Blakey & Kenny Drew with the Modern Jazz Quartet $17.99
00675000 David Sanborn Collection $19.99
00672491 The New Best of Wayne Shorter $24.99
00672550 The Sonny Stitt Collection $19.95
00672524 Lester Young Collection $22.99

TROMBONE

00672332 J.J. Johnson Collection $24.99
00672489 Steve Turré Collection $19.99

TRUMPET

00672557 Herb Alpert Collection $19.99
00672480 Louis Armstrong Collection $22.99
00672481 Louis Armstrong Plays Standards $22.99
00672435 Chet Baker Collection $24.99
00672556 Best of Chris Botti $21.99
00672448 Miles Davis – Originals, Vol. 1 ..... $19.99
00672451 Miles Davis – Originals, Vol. 2 ..... $19.95
00672449 Miles Davis – Standards, Vol. 2 ... $19.95
00672479 Dizzy Gillespie Collection $19.95
00673214 Freddie Hubbard $19.99
00672506 Chuck Mangione Collection $22.99

Visit our web site for songlists or to order online from your favorite music retailer at
www.halleonard.com

Prices, content, and availability subject to change without notice.